NEXT LEVEL

RAISING THE STANDARD OF GRACE

ROBERT GAY

Parsons Publishing House
Stafford, Virginia USA

Next Level—Raising the Standard of Grace
by Robert Gay

Parsons Publishing House
P. O. Box 488
Stafford, VA 22554 USA
www.ParsonsPublishingHouse.com
Info@ParsonsPublishingHouse.com

All Scripture quotations, unless otherwise indicated, are taken from the *New King James Version*® (NKJV). Copyright © 1982 by Thomas Nelson, Inc. Used by permission. All rights reserved.
Scripture quotations marked (KJV) are taken from *Holy Bible, King James Version*.
Scripture quotations marked (ERV) are taken from the *Holy Bible: Easy-to-Read Version*™. Copyright © 1987, 1999, 2006 by World Bible Translation Center, Inc, and used by permission.
Scripture quotations marked (CEV) are taken from the *Contemporary English Bible*, copyright ©1991, 1992, 1995 by the American Bible Society. Used with permission.
Scriptures and additional materials marked (GNB) are quoted are from the *Good News Bible* © 1994 published by the Bible Societies/Harper Collins Publishers Ltd UK, Good News Bible© American Bible Society 1966, 1971, 1976, 1992. Used with permission.

Cover Art: Micah Gay

ISBN -13: 978-1-60273-042-7
ISBN -10: 160273-042-3
Library of Congress Control Number: 2013942711
Printed in the United States of America.
For World-Wide Distribution.

DEDICATION

This book is dedicated to all of the preachers and teachers of the uncompromised Word of Truth, both past and present. There have been those who have gone before us that have carried the flame of God's Word and have cleared and lit a path for all to follow. They were unceasing in their determination to publish and broadcast the gospel in the face of opposition and threats.

Whether they were popular or not, they never flinched in their quest to accomplish the purpose of God. Many gave their lives for the gospel. Many of them never saw full recompense in this life. However, they continued to push forward the declaration of truth.

May their lives be an example for us who are now entrusted with that same Word of Truth. May we carry on their legacy and continue to boldly proclaim the message of spiritual liberty that frees man from the slavery to sin and bondage. Let us be found faithful to speak what God is declaring to our generation and lift up the standard of righteousness.

To all of these men and women, this book is dedicated.

TABLE OF CONTENTS

PREFACE

Several years ago, after pastoring for fourteen years and close to thirty years of full-time ministry involvement, the Lord began to speak to my heart concerning Grace and the Ten Commandments. As a pastor, I had never taught an entire series on the Ten Commandments. As one in ministry, I had never focused much attention on them. I had mentioned them and taught them in related sermons, yet had never focused exclusively on these important directives that God gave to His people.

It seemed that these commands lacked importantance to me. It wasn't that I believed they were to be ignored, because I believed the exact opposite; I believed they were to be observed. It wasn't that I believed they were no longer relevant, because I knew they were all rearticulated in the New Testament. However, the importance of these commands had never really dawned on my heart to the necessary degree.

Most all of us are familiar with the movie that featured Charlton Heston as Moses entitled *The Ten Commandments*. To many, viewing it by today's cinematic standard, it seems a little "cheesy." However, it did bring to light the process of the giving of the ten most important commands that God ever issued to mankind since the fall of Adam.

I must admit regrettably that I had never focused much attention on any of the Ten Commandments because of what I perceived as a spirit of religiosity of which I wanted no part. To be honest with you, they just seemed a little boring and non-exciting. After all, who wants to preach something uninteresting to people? Who wants to spend all their time just ministering a message of "don't do this" and "don't do that"? The unfortunate reality is that I lacked understanding and revelation concerning these most important commandments.

Think about this: God could have commanded His people anything that He so desired. However, there were only ten specific directives that God gave to His people on the tablets of stone that He originally transcribed. It seems to me that if God would take time to engrave these edicts on tablets of stone, then we certainly should place some measure of importance upon them. If these were the ten most important things that God wanted His people to understand, then we certainly should have some kind of grasp of them and hold them in high esteem.

There are many believers today who do not even know the Ten Commandments. Part of the reason for this is that these commandments are not taught in many churches. Some ministers have substituted the teaching and preaching of the Word of God with a "You Can Feel Wonderful" message. These sermons spiritually anesthetize people, but produce no change and long term fruit within their lives. I understand that the gospel is "good news," but it does not mean that a pastor bypasses the teaching of biblical directives so everyone can leave a service merely feeling better about their existence.

Most believers today would be hard pressed to quote five of the Ten Commandments. In the Body of Christ today there is great ignorance concerning these commands. Why? It's because they don't hear them mentioned; they haven't been taught. Pastors need to realize that if they fail to teach these commands, believers will not know them and consequently fail to do them.

The government is not going to teach them because humanism has been the rule of the day. The public school system is not going to teach them because legal rulings have removed them from our schools. So who is charged with that responsibility? Who is going to reinforce what God dictated to Moses as the commandments of His covenant? It should be those who are occupying the pulpits of churches.

As I was praying one day, the Lord began to speak to my heart concerning the relationship between Grace and the Ten Commandments. Unfortunately, some have used the word "grace" to disavow the Ten Commandments. Some have said that these ten directives from the Lord are no longer relevant for those who are in the New Testament. Some have gone so far as to say that the preaching and teaching of the Ten Commandments is bondage.

The reality is that Grace and the Ten Commandments are not at odds with each other. They are actually in perfect agreement. You will see in this book how these commandments do not violate grace. God's moral law did not change in the New Covenant. He is the same yesterday, today, and forever.

Grace is probably one of the most misunderstood and misused words in the church today. Believers have used the word "grace" to excuse all types of behavior. Many have used the word "grace" as an opportunity for fleshly behavior that is displeasing to God. Others have used the word "grace" to justify conduct that is absolutely repulsive.

Some have said that anything that resembles law is unbiblical for believers in the New Testament. They use the word "grace" to condemn the confrontation of sin. They condemn those who confront sin while declaring it is wrong to condemn. I'm sure you can see the hypocrisy of this belief and behavior. It appears the only people that they believe should be condemned are those who shine the light on their sin. Contrariwise, Paul said that we are to expose the unfruitful works of darkness (Ephesians 5:11).

The truth is that the Ten Commandments and Grace are not antagonistic nor opposed. They are not at war with each other. If you believe they are, I encourage you to take a step back and look again.

I believe that in every one of these important commands we can see the heart of the Father God. Every one of them is an expression of His heart and love for us. They are a rendering of His desire for our lives. None of them are meant to make our lives difficult; they are there to keep us from difficulty. For instance: remaining faithful to your spouse does not make your life difficult; it keeps you from difficulty and disaster.

I believe the Lord desires us to examine the Ten Commandments through the eyes of Grace. There is a fresh perspective that He wants to give us that will allow us to live life in greater abundance. We are not looking at these commandments simply on the surface level as a restriction of certain behavior. We are examining them with an understanding of the heart of the Father who intends to produce abundant life within His children.

All of us who are parents gave directives to our children when they were little. If your children were like mine, they may have replied at some time with the question, "Why". Of course, being the wonderful parents that we are, we replied with the answer, "Because I said so." The truth is that should be enough.

Just the fact that you gave a commandment to your children means it should be followed. May I say that we should obey God's commandments just because our Father said it! That should be enough.

However, there are times when it is good for us as parents to explain the purpose of our directives to our children. If we forbid them to play in the street (that was always a big command in our house), then explain to them the dangers and consequences of playing in the street. If we tell them to clean their room, they may exclaim that they can walk in it with no problem. We must make it clear to them the benefits of a clean room and the consequence of a dirty room, whatever that may be in your particular household.

God illuminates to us more than His command. He reveals the purpose and heart for everything He expects of us. We must understand that the commandments that He gave were not for His benefit, but for ours. When we understand His heart in the command, the toil of fulfilling it ceases. When we understand the purpose for the directive, we are then empowered to accomplish it.

It is His grace that empowers. It is grace that enables us to do and fulfill. It is grace that allows us to understand and receive revelation knowledge. My prayer for you is that you will receive these truths as you allow the heart of the Father to be revealed in you.

LIFE AND THE COMMANDMENTS

Now behold, one came and said to Him, "Good Teacher, what good thing shall I do that I may have eternal life?" So He said to him, "Why do you call Me good? No one is good but One, that is, God. But if you want to enter into life, keep the commandments." He said to Him, "Which ones?" Jesus said, "'YOU SHALL NOT MURDER,' 'YOU SHALL NOT COMMIT ADULTERY,' 'YOU SHALL NOT STEAL,' 'YOU SHALL NOT BEAR FALSE WITNESS,' 'HONOR YOUR FATHER AND YOUR MOTHER,' and, 'YOU SHALL LOVE YOUR NEIGHBOR AS YOURSELF'" (Matthew 19:16-19).

The Desire for Life

In this passage of Scripture, we see a man that we refer to as the rich young ruler come to Jesus asking him a very simple question. His question is what needs to be done to experience eternal life. This man desires something that every person wants: eternal life.

On a natural level, life is the most fundamental desire of man. Man has been programmed by his Creator to live. God ordained man to experience His life and that in abundance. Man will fight to live. He will spend money to keep himself alive and fight sickness and disease. He will do everything within his power to experience life.

No one wants eternal death. No one in their right mind is trying to find a way to die. Man looks for ways to prolong his physical life and enjoy it at the same time. The most basic desire of mankind is to continue to live.

As Christians, we realize that eternal life is not merely what we will experience one day in heaven. Eternal life begins at the moment we make Jesus the Lord of our lives. We know that eternal life is the very life of God. It is that which produces fulfillment regardless of situations or circumstances. It is the very life of God that we possess within our spirits.

The Key to Life

In the question posed to Jesus by the rich young ruler, the word that is used for **life** in the original Greek language is **zoe**. It is the same word that is used in the Gospel of John when he said, "In Him (Jesus) was life (zoe), and the life (zoe) was the light of men." *Zoe* is the very life of God. It is the essence of His being and the personification of His character. It is that which can only be received from Him because He is the point of its origin.

Jesus could have given a lot of different answers to the question of what you need to do to experience life. If He had wanted to He could have said you need to pray more. However,

He didn't. He could have said you need to hear the reading of Scripture more often. However, He didn't. In answer to the question Jesus immediately refers back to that which we know as the Ten Commandments.

Jesus told the rich young ruler without blinking an eye that life (*zoe*) begins by keeping the commandments. In light of much of what is being taught in the church today, that is a radical idea. Jesus said that the key to the longing of man and most fundamental desire is to keep God's commandments. Jesus connected LIFE to COMMANDMENTS.

Receiving Jesus and Righteous Behavior

Every problem that we have in our society and culture today is NOT due to people rejecting Jesus as Savior, but rather the rejecting of His commandments. Every murder you see reported, every robbery you hear about, and every lie that is spoken has its roots in the failure to keep God's commandments. Every broken marriage, adulterous affair, and unwanted pregnancy has its roots in the lapse of obedience and adherence to His commands.

Please do not misunderstand me. People need Jesus. He is our Redeemer. However, I've found that more people like Jesus than like His commandments. Many people who say they love Jesus actually despise His commands. Something is wrong with this picture.

Somewhere along the line, we have separated the act of receiving Jesus as our Savior and its connection to godly behavior and conduct. We have taken Scriptures out of context to create doctrines that negate the necessity of righteous behavior and holy living. The discussion of holy living from the pulpits in America is almost non-existent today. Why? Because we are now being told that some may feel condemned if we say anything about sin. We are told that raising a standard of righteousness and holy living is something that is unattainable and will therefore cause many to give up. We are told that the preaching of the Ten Commandments and holy living is "law" and not grace. Obviously, Jesus did not get that memo!

We see in the Bible that Jesus repeatedly referenced and emphasized the keeping of the Ten Commandments while He walked the earth. So when He gave His answer to the question of experiencing life (*zoe*), it cannot be separated from keeping His commandments. In other words, you cannot experience *ZOE* and live in sin at the same time. Willful disobedience to God's commandments will produce death and destruction whether you are saved or not.

With this being said, we must understand the Ten Commandments are still applicable for us today. Grace does not abolish these directives and they are still to be practiced.

> Then one of them, a lawyer, asked Him a question, testing Him, and saying, "Teacher, which is the great commandment in the law?" Jesus said to him, "'YOU SHALL LOVE THE LORD YOUR GOD WITH ALL YOUR HEART, WITH ALL YOUR SOUL, AND WITH ALL YOUR MIND.' This is the first and great commandment. And the second is like it: 'YOU SHALL LOVE YOUR NEIGHBOR AS YOURSELF.' On these two commandments hang all the Law and the Prophets" (Matthew 22:35-40).

Once again, Jesus is asked a question that involves an answer related to the Law and Commandments. I think that it is interesting to note that Jesus had plenty of opportunity to negate any type of adherence to any of the commandments. Jesus could have said that there was a new day of grace coming when it would not matter how you behaved and sin would be acceptable. But, He didn't! He could have said that it is unimportant to possess any kind of standard of righteousness and we should tolerate and accept sin as the norm. However, He didn't! Jesus answers this question by referring to what the Jews recognized as the foundation of moral law.

The Two Tablets

The Ten Commandments were divided into two tablets. We see this written in Exodus 34:

> *So he was there with the LORD forty days and forty nights; he neither ate bread nor drank water. And He wrote on the tablets the words of the covenant, the Ten Commandments. Now it was so, when Moses came down from Mount Sinai (and the two tablets of the Testimony were in Moses' hand when he came down from the mountain) (Exodus 34:28-29).*

Most theologians agree that the first tablet pertained to loving God and the second to loving mankind. The first half of the Ten Commandments contained issues dealing with man's relationship and love expressed toward God. Likewise, the second half were relating to the same with mankind. Therefore, Jesus was by His answer referencing back to the Ten Commandments once again.

This is why the Apostle Paul later says that the last five commandments are fulfilled when you love your neighbor as yourself.

> *For the commandments, "YOU SHALL NOT COMMIT ADULTERY," "YOU SHALL NOT MURDER," "YOU SHALL NOT STEAL," "YOU SHALL NOT BEAR FALSE WITNESS," "YOU SHALL NOT COVET," and if there is any other commandment, are all summed up in this saying, namely, "YOU SHALL LOVE YOUR NEIGHBOR AS YOURSELF" (Romans 13:9).*

Paul articulates an understanding that was had by Jewish theologians. The expression of obedience to the first tablet equaled loving God. The expression of obedience to the second tablet equaled loving your neighbor. This was a basic principle that was understood by Jews. Understand that there is no fulfilling of any law if that law does not exist. So when Paul says that love fulfills the Ten Commandments, it means they are in existence and are to be fulfilled.

All the Law and Prophets

Jesus goes so far as to say that the entire law hangs on the fulfillment of two commandments which are actually the fulfillment of all the Ten Commandments. That doesn't sound to me as if Jesus is diminishing the importance of the Ten Commandments. If anything, He is emphasizing and placing importance on them.

What a powerful statement from Jesus: all the law and prophets hang on these commands. At that time, the law and prophets was the Word of God. The purpose for the written Word was to ensure that commandments were followed. The writings of the prophets revealed the necessity that these commands be obeyed.

God would send prophets to bring repentance to the nation of Israel. "Why?" It was because they had disobeyed these commandments. God would send and permit judgment. "Why?" It was because they had not fulfilled these commandments. It was fairly simple. Obey God's commands and receive His blessing. Disobey God's commands and receive the curse. It was not complicated; God never made it difficult to understand.

The Ten Commandments Today

What is very interesting is that our entire system of law within our nation today was originally based on the Ten Commandments. Many of the Founding Fathers of the United

States made statements concerning the necessity of the Ten Commandments within a society. They said that a society or government could not last or survive without their implementation. Some went on to say that anarchy would be the end result if these laws were not followed.

Today, the Ten Commandments are depicted in the Supreme Court of the United States, our National Archives, and many other government buildings. Is it possible that the men who originally posted these had some understanding of their importance? Is it possible that they had actually read the words of Jesus where His prescription for life was to keep the commandments? Do you think that perhaps they had an understanding that the church needs to be reminded of today?

I recognize that words posted on a plaque or on doors have no power by themselves. However, it does make a statement for what should be the basis of government and the rule of law. It makes a declaration that the foundation of law begins with adherence to the Ten Commandments.

In recent years, there has been debate over the Ten Commandments and their role in civil government and law. We have seen monuments that contained the Ten Commandments removed from state buildings. We have seen and heard of them being taken down from the view of children in classrooms. The argument has been that some may be offended and (as ridiculous as it may sound) might obey them. God forbid that the children in our schools would actually read and obey the Ten Commandments. What an awful world we would have if children no longer lied or stole. I say this sarcastically. This is the insanity that is now touted as just rulings from our courts.

But really, is it any wonder that these commandments have been dishonored in this manner? Is it any wonder that we have had some of the traumatic events within our schools? Is it any wonder that many things have gone awry? Could it be that when we start removing God's law we remove His protection?

Could it be that when we refuse His commands we forsake His mercy?

In the Church Today

In the church over the last several decades there has been an eroding away from the teaching of anything that could be considered "law." We are being told that to be saved we must merely believe with no expectation being placed upon the believer in regards to holy living. Some are even teaching that all roads lead to heaven, and at the end of the day, we are going to be just one happy family in heaven. Many go on to say, it doesn't matter how you live as long as you don't hurt anybody.

A close study of the Bible reveals that these are false doctrines and false teachings that are producing a lukewarm church that is full of sin. I say this not to condemn, but rather as a spiritual alarm that I believe God is sounding today. It is time for those who say they are Christians, but are acting like the world in their manner of living, to repent and change their ways.

New Understanding of Grace

We must understand that grace never exempts anyone from the requirement of righteous living. Jesus never said to live however you want to live. The Apostle Paul never promoted a lifestyle that was free from the boundaries established by the Ten Commandments. Grace is not merely a covering for sin that gives you a "hall pass" to live according to the dictates of the flesh. Nothing could be further from the truth.

Grace is God's divine ability. Grace gives us power to fulfill the commandments. Grace enables us to live above sin. Grace enables us to do through the power of God what those under the law could not do by themselves. The law revealed sin, but grace causes righteousness to be revealed. Grace will cause holy living to be realized within our lives.

Law Written Upon the Heart

"Behold, the days are coming, says the LORD, when I will make a new covenant with the house of Israel and with the house of Judah—not according to the covenant that I made with their fathers in the day that I took them by the hand to lead them out of the land of Egypt, My covenant which they broke, though I was a husband to them, says the LORD. But this is the covenant that I will make with the house of Israel after those days, says the LORD: I will put My law in their minds, and write it on their hearts; and I will be their God, and they shall be My people" (Jeremiah 31:31-33).

Jeremiah declares that there is a new day coming. The Lord says that He will make a covenant with His people unlike the one He made with them in the giving of the Ten Commandments. He continues on to describe how this will be different. God says, "I will put my law in their minds, and write it on their hearts."

God did not say that His law would change. Rather, the location of the transcription would change. He says that in this covenant He will write the law on their hearts. What the Lord is saying is that the law will no longer be an external law which is imposed, but rather an internal law that motivates. Whereas, God wrote it originally on tablets of stone, it is now going to be written on the heart of man. He said that He would write His law, not His suggestion.

In actuality, the tablets of stone were a prophetic depiction of that which God would do within the heart of man. God had already laid out a plan that He was enacting. He already knew that Jesus would come to the earth and create a way whereby all mankind could have the law of God written on their hearts. Paul said we were known in Christ before the foundation of the world (Ephesians 1:4). Jesus coming to pay the price for the sin of mankind was not plan B; it was in the mind of God from the start.

So we see this comparative contrast that Jeremiah is speaking by the Holy Spirit. He says that just as the law was written on stone, God now writes it on hearts. He says the change is where, not what! The change is not the law of God, but rather where it's being written.

Inseparable Internal Law

Let me make a bold statement now. Christians are still under law! Wow! What a contrast from what we hear today. However, the law we are under is an internal law that has been written. It is a law that has been carved on the tablet of your heart. Yet, it is still law.

Being a Christian does not mean that you are free from law. It means that you are now enabled to fulfill it. Being born again does not mean that you can live however you want to live. It means that you can live holy because you are now programmed internally to obey. The moment you are born of the Spirit (born again) you come under the law of the Spirit. That law initiates obedience to God's moral law which is found in the Ten Commandments.

We see this principle in the comparison that Jeremiah articulates. Moses wrote the covenant on the tablets of stone. The covenant that was on the tablets of stone were the Ten Commandments (Exodus 24:28). That means this: the New Covenant DOES NOT separate us from the Ten Commandments, but rather REINFORCES THEM. It actually brands them in your heart! It takes them to a higher level and dimension.

In the Old Covenant it was the law of the covenant written on stone. In the New Covenant it is still the law of the covenant, but written on the heart of those who believe in Jesus. Redemption through the blood of Jesus in no way separates us from the moral law that God gave to mankind that was originally contained in the Ten Commandments. The reality is that now the ability to obey and fulfill these commands has been given, and we are without excuse if we choose to live in sin and walk in disobedience.

Jesus said that the key to experiencing His life starts with obedience to God's commandments. The choice is ours. We can obey and be blessed, or we can disobey and reap the consequences. I encourage you to obey.

CHAPTER TWO
HIGHER LEVEL

"Do not think that I came to destroy the Law or the Prophets. I did not come to destroy but to fulfill. For assuredly, I say to you, till heaven and earth pass away, one jot or one tittle will by no means pass from the law till all is fulfilled. Whoever therefore breaks one of the least of these commandments, and teaches men so, shall be called least in the kingdom of heaven; but whoever does and teaches them, he shall be called great in the kingdom of heaven. For I say to you, that unless your righteousness exceeds the righteousness of the scribes and Pharisees, you will by no means enter the kingdom of heaven."

"You have heard that it was said to those of old, 'YOU SHALL NOT MURDER, and whoever murders will be in danger of the judgment.' But I say to you that whoever is angry with his brother without a cause shall be in danger of the judgment. And whoever says to his *brother, 'Raca!' shall be in danger of the council. But whoever says, 'You fool!' shall be in danger of hell fire. "*

"You have heard that it was said to those of old, 'YOU SHALL NOT COMMIT ADULTERY.' But I say to you that whoever looks at a woman to lust for her has already committed adultery with her in his heart. "

"Again you have heard that it was said to those of old, 'You shall not swear falsely, but shall perform your oaths to the Lord.' But I say to you, do not swear at all: neither by heaven, for it is God's throne; nor by the earth, for it is His footstool; nor by Jerusalem, for it is the city of the great King. Nor shall you swear by your head, because you cannot make one hair white or black. But let your 'Yes' be 'Yes,' and your 'No,' 'No.' For whatever is more than these is from the evil one. "

"You have heard that it was said, 'YOU SHALL LOVE YOUR NEIGHBOR and hate your enemy.' But I say to you, love your enemies, bless those who curse you, do good to those who hate you, and pray for those who spitefully use you and persecute you" (Matthew 5:17-22, 27-28, 33-37, 43-44).

This is a wonderful passage of Scripture. Jesus is teaching a message that we call the Sermon on the Mount. He has just given the Beatitudes (I like to refer to them as the attitudes you should be). Then, Jesus begins to share how we are the light of the world and the salt of the earth. Immediately on the heels of that, He starts talking about the law. More specifically he starts a discourse on moral law and the Ten Commandments.

He starts by basically saying that He did not come to do away with the law or the prophets. There is another place that Jesus refers to the law and the prophets when He answers the question concerning the greatest commandment. His answer was that the entire law and prophets hang on the two commandments that are actually the fulfillment of all of the Ten Commandments. So, when Jesus starts His discourse by saying He didn't come to destroy the law or the prophets, He in essence declares that the Ten Commandments are not going away. That's right! The Ten Commandments have not passed away. They are still relevant!

Another thing that Jesus points out is the importance of both obeying the commandments and teaching them. He also poses a warning to anyone who would attempt to teach someone to break any of the Ten Commandments or do so themselves. He says they would be considered the least in the kingdom of God. Jesus praises the ones who would teach and obey with the promise of greatness and warns any who would do differently. That's what Jesus said.

Jesus then proceeds to talk about several of these commandments we find in the Ten Commandments. It is possible that He discussed more than the ones mentioned and it was not recorded. But we know He talked specifically about three of them and then the commandment of loving your neighbor which encompasses the last five commands contained in the ten.

Jesus Raises the Bar

As Jesus begins to teach on the commandments, He contrasts that which had been taught to that which He is teaching. Let's look at the **first** one to which He refers. Jesus says that you have heard that you are not to murder anyone. But now He says you can't be angry without a cause. Is Jesus changing the commandment? Absolutely Not!

There are two things that are happening. First of all, Jesus is taking the commandment to a higher level of fulfillment. Under the letter of the law you cannot murder. Under grace you can't be angry without cause. You must walk in love and forgiveness. Grace does not diminish the requirement of the commandment, it raises the bar! Grace now takes it to a higher level.

The reality is that the first murder was committed because of anger and hostility. Cain was angry at Abel over God's rejection of his sacrifice while Abel's was accepted. It made him livid; it ultimately drove him to murder.

This leads me to the **second** thing that Jesus is communicating. He is now dealing with the root of the commandment. Jesus is revealing the heart of the Father within the commandment. We could also say the purposed effect of the commandment on the heart. Jesus was bringing a greater understanding of that which the Father wanted to deal with from the start. Murder is not an issue if there is no anger and hatred. Jesus was declaring 'refrain from being angry and you won't murder.'

In later chapters, we will discuss all of these commandments and how Jesus would get to the root of them. He expressed the heart of the Father in the commandments. The heart of the commandment was greater than the letter of the law. The root of all the commandments is God's love for us, our love for Him, and our love for one another. However, He never negated any of the Ten Commandments. Jesus did not lower the bar, rather He raised it higher.

The Issues of the Heart

As Jesus begins to talk about the commandment concerning adultery, He once again raises the bar. He says, 'You've heard that you are not to be sleeping around with anyone to whom you are not married (which is adultery). But, now I'm telling you don't look that way.' Once again Jesus is dealing with the heart of the commandment which was not just the physical act of sex outside of marriage, but also that which preceded it. Lust in the heart of man is the problem. Don't do things to feed the lust of the flesh.

So once again Jesus is raising the bar. The commandment is not ceasing, but He is dealing with the root. He's speaking to the heart of the commandment. He is saying that adultery does not begin at the commencement of the illicit physical relationship. It begins when people start looking with sexual desire. Jesus explains that the act of adultery and murder is not the root of the problem; it is lust, unfaithfulness, anger, and hatred that are the issues. These are issues of the heart.

The good news today is that Jesus came to deal with these issues of the heart. He came so we could be born again and become a new creation in Christ Jesus. He did not come to dismantle moral law encased in commandments that had been given. He came to empower us to fulfill that which had already been stated.

Again, Jesus in no way diminished any of the Ten Commandments. He didn't say, 'That's law and is no longer relevant, so live how you want to live.' He said the exact opposite. He emphasized the importance of abiding by the moral law contained within the Ten Commandments.

Reciprocating Love

I'm convinced that a lot of Christians today do not obey the Ten Commandments because they miss the heart of the commandment. We must understand that God was not attempting to "cramp our style." He did not want to mandate behavior that you had no power to fulfill, thus making you feel like a failure for your entire life. Every commandment that is contained in the Ten Commandments is rooted in reciprocating love. That means the commandment was given through His love for us and is fulfilled through our love for Him and our neighbor.

There are some that have taught that to love is the only command. While I will agree that if we walk in love, we will fulfill all of the Ten Commandments; it does not mean that love is the only relevant commandment. It means the commandments are still relevant and to be obeyed, but now we have a way through the grace of God for every one of them to be fulfilled. Love cannot fulfill a law if it doesn't exist. You cannot fill a glass with water if there is not a glass to fill. His grace is sufficient and will be enough to empower us to do what God has mandated.

We must understand that the grace of God does not liberate us from the commandments. Grace empowers us to fulfill them. Grace does not liberate you from biblical moral law, but rather gives you the ability to be the open demonstration of Christ in the earth. Grace is not demonstrated by freedom from law, but rather submission and obedience to it. Grace empowers us to now fulfill these commandments from a heart that has been made new. Grace deals with the root of the problem, that being the heart of man.

There is therefore now no condemnation to those who are in Christ Jesus, who do not walk according to the flesh, but according to the Spirit. For the law of the Spirit of life in Christ Jesus has made me free from the law of sin and death. For what the law could not do in that it was weak through the flesh, God did by sending His own Son in the likeness of sinful flesh, on account of sin: He condemned sin in the flesh, that the righteous requirement of the law might be fulfilled in us who do not walk according to the flesh but according to the Spirit (Romans 8:1-4).

Misunderstanding in the Church

This passage of Scripture has been quoted and preached a tremendous amount. There have also been songs written from these Scriptures. However, there is little comprehension and understanding of what Paul is fully communicating. You can determine this by the way that many believers use this passage of Scripture.

I have known of people to live in sin and then quote this Scripture. There are those who have taken this verse to mean that since they are saved, there is no condemnation for any sin in which they choose to participate. They believe that somehow they are exempt from behavioral responsibility as it applies to righteous living. It is as if they have been given a "sin pass."

Many times these same people begin to say that if a minister preaches a standard of righteous living and says anything that confronts sinful behavior that he is a minister of condemnation. If that were true, Jesus was a minister of condemnation. Jesus preached a standard of righteous living. Jesus preached against sin and told people to STOP SINNING! Paul told the people who were thieves to STOP STEALING!

When Jesus and Paul confronted sin there were two things happening. **First** of all, there was an identification of sin. Some people sin today because they lack the understanding that what they are doing is wrong. It needs to be identified. The **second** thing is there was a directive of change given. When Jesus told the woman caught in adultery to stop sinning, it was a command for her to change. We hear a lot of preaching on the words of Jesus when He said, "Neither do I condemn you." However, we hear very little about "go and sin no more," which paraphrased is STOP SINNING!

A Christian should never use any Scripture in the Bible to try to argue for their right to sin or even get close to it. I do not believe the Apostle Paul anticipated that a letter written to the church at Rome would be used to excuse and justify sinful behavior. I do not believe that he ever anticipated that carnal believers would use grace as a crutch for the failure to change their lives and turn from wickedness. Those who have interpreted Romans 8:1 in this manner are mistaken.

There is a qualifying statement that Paul brings to light at the end of this verse. He says, "Who do not walk according to the flesh, but according to the Spirit." What does that mean? It simply means to those who DO NOT SIN! This is not real complicated. It's fairly simple. Walking free from sin keeps you free from condemnation. Paul is saying that we can live free from condemnation once we are saved if we will choose to walk in the Spirit and not in the flesh.

In Galatians 5, Paul articulates the works of the flesh. These are the works of sin. These are the byproducts of the natural appetites and tendency of the body coupled with the carnal mind. These are things that Paul commands believers to avoid and flee. These are the things that the Bible calls sin and are to be shunned by those who call themselves Christians. Grace does not excuse walking in the flesh.

There is one key verse that many people miss when they read this passage of Scripture found in Romans 8. That is verse four which says:

"That the righteous requirement of the law might be fulfilled in us who do not walk according to the flesh but according to the Spirit" *(Romans 8:4).*

There are several things I want to point out in this Scripture. The first is the phrase: "righteous requirement of the law." Paul was saying that there is still a requirement of moral law that is to be fulfilled. The whole reason that we were born again and now have the indwelling presence of the Holy Spirit is so that we can meet the requirement of the law. Paul is speaking specifically of moral law in this passage.

Two Portions of the Law

Understand that the law was broken up into two portions. There was moral law that had its basis in the Ten Commandments about which we have been discussing. There was also Levitical ceremonial law. Some have referred to it as priestly law. This had to do with the offering of sacrifices, feasts, circumcision, washing instructions, etc. Once and for all, Jesus fulfilled the Levitical law when He willingly offered himself as a sacrifice. There is nothing more that is required for salvation.

When we read the book of Hebrews, it reveals in detail how Jesus accomplished everything. We see a marvelous discourse on how the shed blood of Jesus took care of it all. We now look at the things involved in ceremonial law as types and shadows of that which Jesus came to do and successfully accomplished.

However, concerning moral law, it is restated in the New Testament. Whereas the ceremonial law has clearly been done away with in the New Covenant, the moral law has clearly been rearticulated. Unfortunately, many have confused the two and interpreted freedom from law as freedom from godly behavior. The law that we are free from is Levitical ceremonial law, not moral law that has its basis in the Ten Commandments.

The Commandments Restated

There is no place where Paul ever indicates that we are to ignore the Ten Commandments. He actually restates them all in one way or another. If Paul is going to refer back to the Ten Commandments repeatedly in his writings, it seems logical to think that he did not believe or teach that we are exempt from their fulfillment.

Why would Paul quote the fifth commandment of "honor your father and mother" to the Ephesians and remind them of the promise associated with it if not applicable to us today? Why would Paul also tell those who were stealing to stop it, which is actually the eighth commandment, if it was not relevant? Why would Paul, if we are not under law, rearticulate these commandments? The answer is obvious. We are not free from moral law or the Ten Commandments!

If the Apostle Paul was trying to say that there is no obligation for Christians to obey the Ten Commandments then we would have to conclude that he was talking out of both sides of his mouth. We would also need to rip the book of James out of our Bible because he repeated the necessity of righteous works and godly behavior. James went so far as to say that it requires more than belief alone to be saved and that holiness is an equal part that bears witness of salvation.

The Law of the Spirit

Another thing I would like to point out is that Paul begins to refer to the law of the Spirit. He is contrasting the law that was written with the law of the Spirit. One thing you can see from this is that there is still a LAW to which we are to be subject, that being the law of the Spirit. When we obey the LAW of the Spirit, we will fulfill the written moral law, in particular the Ten Commandments. They are not at odds with each other. It's not one or the other because they agree.

The law of the Spirit is the law that has been written on your spirit man—your heart. It is the law that the Holy Spirit empowers us to fulfill. It is not a different moral law. But, the location is now within our spirit man rather than two tablets of stone.

I believe we are living in a season of time when we need to hear once again the necessity of living by the Ten Commandments. This does not mean we are going back under legalism, but rather we are receiving an understanding of that which is now required that can only be performed with the aid of the Holy Spirit. It will help us maintain freedom and deliverance within our lives.

Sin—The Doorway of Satan

You must understand that sin is the door through which Satan enters. The Bible declares to us that the enemy could find no place in Jesus. This was because He was the sinless Son of God who walked victoriously over temptation. He never succumbed to any enticement that Satan threw at Him. He walked in righteousness and holiness. The writer of Hebrews says that Jesus was exalted because He loved righteousness and hated iniquity.

One issue we have in the church today is that many believers no longer hate sin. Many have been taught to "tolerate" and put up with it. Obviously, Jesus did not receive that teaching. Perhaps because He was the Word and knew better than to fall prey to that kind of false doctrine!

Today we have those who declare they are Christians, but live like every other unbeliever while they go around saying, 'Don't hate on me, I'm just a sinner saved by grace.' Are they a sinner? It definitely appears that way based on how they are living. Are they saved? Perhaps. Are they living by grace? Absolutely not!

Divine Empowerment

Grace means divine ability or empowerment. Living by grace will empower you to live holy. God's grace does not empower you to sin. It enables you to live above it. Paul stated it is by the Holy Spirit that we are now empowered to fulfill the requirement of the commandments. He did not say the Holy Spirit has exempted us from them. Grace echoes the requirement and then gives us the ability to fulfill it.

I want to make sure that you understand that the only way anyone can be saved is through faith in the redemptive work that Jesus accomplished at Calvary. Works will not and cannot save you. It is by faith in Jesus alone. However, this does not mean we are in some way or another exempt from holy living. We are actually more responsible because we have God's ability to fulfill the "righteous requirement of the law" through the Holy Spirit. That is what Paul said.

Free From Bondage

When we look at Exodus 20, we see something that I think is very interesting:

"And God spoke all these words, saying: 'I am the LORD your God, who brought you out of the land of Egypt, out of the house of bondage'" (Exodus 20:1-2).

This is what immediately precedes the giving of the Ten Commandments. God says, 'I have brought you out of the land of Egypt and out of the house of bondage.' Most all theologians believe, as it is borne out in the New Testament, Egypt is a type and shadow for sin. Egypt is a type of the unregenerate man. God bringing the children of Israel out of Egypt is a type for someone being set free from sin at the moment of salvation.

So we see God has liberated Israel and set them free. We see that God Himself is declaring that He has brought them out of the house of bondage. They have been emancipated. Then the very next thing that God utters is the Ten Commandments.

There are several things I would like for you to think about. The first is that I believe this is a type of what happens to us at salvation. What we see happening here is indicative of that which takes place when someone accepts Jesus as their Savior. When we are born again, God writes His law upon our hearts.

Being saved does not mean we are free from law, but that the law is now written on the inside of us. Just as God liberated Israel and then gave them these commandments, when we are saved there are commandments that are given. Our responsibility increases at the time of salvation. We are not to live flippantly because we have been redeemed and are now the righteousness of God in Christ Jesus. We actually assume a greater responsibility as to the way we conduct our lives.

The second thing I want you to think about is this. If the Ten Commandments are bondage, as many say, why did God make a point to say that He had delivered them from the house of bondage and then turn around and dictate commandments? Why did He not say, 'I've changed the type of bondage you're in' if moral law was bondage? Does it make sense that God would deliver His people from bondage (Egypt) to only bring them into it again through the giving of moral law? If living by the Ten Commandments is, as some would say, "not living by faith", then why would God, who cannot be pleased outside of faith, give them in the first place? Was God deliberately trying to ensnare the people that He had just delivered?

Freedom through Obedience

Let it be known that God's Ten Commandments are not bondage. If you obey them, they will produce life and freedom. Living by the Ten Commandments requires you to live by faith because that is the way you fulfill them.

God did not bring His people out of Egyptian bondage only to imprison them with the giving of commandments. He was showing them a way that they could remain free. Following the Ten Commandments is a way to maintain freedom and liberty within your life.

Let's look at this purely from a natural perspective. If you are convicted of stealing, you will go to prison. If you are convicted of murder, you will go to prison and possibly be executed. If you are convicted of perjury as a result of lying in court, you may go to jail. Does that sound like freedom to you? Freedom comes as the result of obedience, not disobedience to law.

If there is something inherently wrong with the Ten Commandments, and they are in some way bondage, then every civil law we have derived from them is wrong. As Christians, we should be protesting the laws against murder because they are bondage. I say this sarcastically to help you see that this line of thinking, that the Ten Commandments are bondage, is absolutely ridiculous!

God gave these commandments because they are keys to staying free. If you follow them, you will be blessed and live in freedom. If you violate them, you will be ensnared and live in bondage.

It is time that we begin to look at the Ten Commandments from a place of grace. It is time that we realize that grace empowers us to fulfill them at a higher level. The grace of God now enables us to do what can only be done through the Spirit of the Lord. We can function on a higher level because of God's grace and His Spirit that empower us.

CHAPTER THREE
THE PRIORITY OF LIFE

"You shall have no other gods before Me."
(Exodus 20:3)

One of the things that I desire to share in this book is that there is an underlying principle contained within each of the Ten Commandments that is more than just the "you shall not" that is found in the written commandment. This is not to add to any commandment or to take away from it, but rather to bring a greater understanding about the heart of the Father when He gave the commandment. These underlying principles along with the commandments themselves are carried over into the New Testament.

Jesus took the commandments to a higher dimension. He brought greater understanding as He taught them. Jesus raised the bar and the standard for every commandment that He discussed. The reason for this is that He understood the heart of the commandment.

Put Me First

The very first commandment that God gives to His people is that they are to have no other gods before Him. Another way to say this in the affirmative is PUT ME FIRST. In other words God was declaring, 'Make Me the priority of your life.'

The first commandment is first for a reason. It is the foundation for all others. It is the priority. It is the most important because if you miss this one you will ultimately fail in the rest. Living for Him begins by making Him the priority.

We live in a day when many people place anything and everything in a position of greater importance than God. Many believers will say that God is the priority of their life, yet never crack their Bibles, spend time in prayer, or even think about God unless they are in trouble. Then, they call out to Him.

For so many, God is nothing more than fire insurance from hell and the one on whom they call to rescue them from their own poor decisions. He is a distant acquaintance that they may mention when they pray over their meal. They may even attend His house when it is convenient and doesn't interfere with any of their other planned activities. However, their daily lifestyles declare that God is far from their thinking.

Making Him the priority of life means that you love Him more than anything else. You love Him more than the air you breathe and the food you eat. It means that your heart and passion is to follow Him. It means that career and money are not more important than Him. It means that pleasure and entertainment are not more important than Him. It means that you are running after Him. He is your life!

This is the bottom line: if we don't get this one right, we will get the others wrong. If we fail at this one, we will fail at the others. God's first command is to make Him the priority and passion of our lives.

The Most Important Thing

The most important thing that you will ever do in this life is PUT JESUS FIRST. If He's not first, then He is not at all. He will not have any gods before Him. There is only one seat that He desires. That is the seat of number one. He cannot and will not live in a secondary position.

There are a lot of things today that can distract us from the most important commandment. Most of them are not necessarily bad within themselves. However, the enemy will use good things to distract us from that which is most important. For the most part, the devil does not try to use evil things to cause believers to sin; he uses things that are good to distract us from that which is God.

For example, a job and career are both good things. We are even commanded in the Bible to work and be productive. We are told to be diligent and do a good job for our employers. However, when job and career begins to be that which drives our lives and it takes the number one seat, then it becomes sin. That doesn't mean you should quit your job. But rather, there needs to be an adjustment in your perspective, attitude, and relationship with it.

A job becoming more important than your relationship with the Lord becomes idolatrous. A career becoming the primary goal of your being is nothing short of breaking the most important command that God gave to His people. Although job and career are good, without proper biblical boundaries and perspective they can become a snare to your soul. This is how many today become workaholics resulting in the loss of their families and everything that is of real importance.

This could be said of anything—whether it is good or bad. Anything that takes the number one position in your life, other than God, will ultimately bring destruction.

God repeatedly said that He was a jealous God. He would not allow His people to put Him in the back seat. Think about that. It is very dishonoring to put Jesus in the back seat of your life. This is the question I have: do you want Him to lead you or do you want to be in front of Him? If you put Him in the back seat, you will be void of guidance. If you put Him in front, He leads and you are afforded guidance. What do you want?

God First Filter

My wife and I have three wonderful children. They are all serving the Lord today and actively involved in ministry. One thing that we always taught our children was to put Jesus first in their lives. Every decision to be made had to go through the "God first filter." If it was going to take them to a place where their relationship and responsibility to God would be negatively affected, then the answer was clear. Jesus must always be first.

Once again, serving God is not complicated. It starts with putting Him first. It is the first commandment because it is the most important. When you put Him first, things begin to fall into place. His yoke is easy and His burden is light. When you put Him first, striving ceases.

This is the bottom line: it's not about me, it's about Him. Paul said, "In Him we live and move and have our being" (Acts 17:28). When you receive this understanding, everything changes. We begin to live our lives from the position that we are here to live for Him.

I think most Christians live from the perspective that He is living just for them. If we need help we can call on Him. If we need healing we can call on Him. While these statements are true, He doesn't want to ONLY be a rescuer in the time of trouble. I do not believe that God wants to be seen like some "super hero" that flies in when you are in a desperate situation while you consistently have a superficial relationship with Him. He wants a relationship with you that can only be achieved when you make Him the priority of your life. He wants to be Numero Uno.

Loving Him the Most

Understand that the priority of your life is dictated by that which you love the most. I think it's very interesting that Jesus said, "If you love me, keep my commandments" (John 14:15). Could it be that the reason God said to make Him the priority of our lives is because loving Him greater than anything else would cause the other commandments to be fulfilled? I believe so.

Loving God more than anything else will cause Him to be the priority and passion of your life. That priority and passion will begin to dictate how we act. That priority will begin to settle decisions that have to be made. That passion will start establishing godly behavioral patterns within our lives.

Operating in Covenant

"Therefore do not worry, saying, 'What shall we eat?' or 'What shall we drink?' or 'What shall we wear?' For after all these things the Gentiles seek. For your heavenly Father knows that you need all these things. But seek first the kingdom of God and His righteousness, and all these things shall be added to you" (Matthew 6:31-33).

In this passage of Scripture Jesus identifies how worry, care, and preoccupation with the things of life can cause someone to go after the wrong thing. We could also say it like this: make the wrong thing the priority of their life. He says that the Gentiles (those without covenant) prioritize food, drink, and clothing. However, Jesus says that we are to make the kingdom of God the priority.

Jesus brings a contrast to the behavior of those who are outside of covenant and those who have a covenant. He says that those who are operating outside of a covenant with God seek the wrong thing. The truth is when we fail to put God first we are behaving like those who are outside of covenant. If we seek after the things of the world, we are acting like those who are without covenant.

Jesus points out that those who live outside of a covenant with God fail to put God first. I believe it is fair to say that Jesus is talking about those who are unsaved. We recognize that people are either saved or unsaved. You are either a part of the kingdom of God or not. Since we who are Christians are a part of God's kingdom, we should make the King first within our lives.

Once again, this is why the first commandment is relevant for us today. If we put other things first, we behave as those who have no covenant. We as Christians have a covenant with God. Therefore, we should act like it. This starts with us making Him the priority of our lives and seeking Him. Failure to do this emphatically shouts, "I am without covenant."

I would like to draw your attention to the word "first" found in verse thirty-three of the previous passage of Scripture. Jesus says to "seek FIRST the kingdom of God and His righteousness, and all these other things will be added." Jesus is saying that these things are going to take care of themselves. You don't have to go after them. They will come on you as the byproduct of putting Him first. Blessing will chase you down if you will start making Him the priority and passion of your life.

Jesus Reinforces the First Commandment

Understand that when Jesus talks about the kingdom of God, it is the domain which belongs to GOD. It is the kingdom which God possesses. The kingdom of God is the rule and dominion of God Almighty. It is the dimension in which God reigns supreme. Now concerning the kingdom, you cannot have a kingdom without a KING. So you cannot seek first the kingdom without making the KING first within your life. Jesus is the KING of the kingdom and must be the priority of your life.

In this passage of Scripture, Jesus is basically saying, "Put me first." "Make me the priority of your life." To seek first the kingdom of God means that you have made the Lord the priority of your life. Jesus is in essence rearticulating the first commandment which states, "Do not have any gods before me." Jesus was reinforcing the first commandment given in the Ten Commandments.

Every commandment that God gives to His people has an overarching principle. It is not merely the words themselves, but there is an underlying spiritual principle that governs. In other words, the spiritual principle that is contained in the command of "you shall have no other gods before me" can also be articulated as, "Put me FIRST." The reason for this is because it means the exact same thing.

The reason I am saying this is to show how that every one of the Ten Commandments are rearticulated in the New Testament, either verbatim or through the overarching principle that governs the commandment. Here we see Jesus doing it. He restates the essence of the first commandment by saying, "Seek first the kingdom of God and His righteousness."

The Motivation of the Command

I want you to see God's motivation for this command. Jesus makes it very clear when He says "all these things will be added to you." God's motivation is His desire to bless you. He wants His children to have their heart's desire. He said that we would be the head and not the tail, above and not beneath (Deuteronomy 28:13).

So the reason for the command is not that we have an egotistical Father who wants to be the center of attention so His opinion of Himself can be exalted. It is so we will look to Him who is the source of all provision. Looking and seeking provision in the wrong place will cause you to come up empty. Understand that His provision is not just financial. It involves every area of your life: spirit, soul, and body.

Notice that Jesus says things will be ADDED as opposed to taken away. Making Him first within your life does not diminish you; it causes you to experience increase. Revelation alert: increase is better than decrease!

The goal of the first commandment is to ultimately produce the blessing of the Lord within our lives. Why would we refuse a command that ends up with the production of prosperity? Why would anyone say that the commandments are bondage when following them will keep you free? My friend, we need to embrace the command to "have no other gods before me" by putting Jesus first within our lives.

First Love – First Priority

"To the angel of the church of Ephesus write, 'These things says He who holds the seven stars in His right hand, who walks in the midst of the seven golden lampstands: "I know your works, your labor, your patience, and that you cannot bear those who are evil.

33

And you have tested those who say they are apostles and are not, and have found them liars; and you have persevered and have patience, and have labored for My name's sake and have not become weary. Nevertheless I have this against you, that you have left your first love. Remember therefore from where you have fallen; repent and do the first works, or else I will come to you quickly and remove your lampstand from its place—unless you repent. But this you have, that you hate the deeds of the Nicolaitans, which I also hate. He who has an ear, let him hear what the Spirit says to the churches. To him who overcomes I will give to eat from the tree of life, which is in the midst of the Paradise of God'" (Revelation 2:1-7).

The believers at Ephesus were participating in and practicing a tremendous amount of wonderful things. They were working and laboring for the kingdom of God. They hated iniquity. They were exercising their spiritual senses and using discernment to prove the true and false apostles. They were perseverant in their work and labor to further the gospel and exalt the name of Jesus.

If most churches today had all these things happening, they would be convinced that revival had arrived. However, Jesus said that He had something against them. That was this: they had left their first love.

I know there are a tremendous amount of messages that have been preached from this passage of Scripture. Some wonderful expositions have been done. But I want to make this very simple. Your first love is your first priority. Priorities are dictated by that which you love more.

Jesus was articulating that they had lost the first priority and passion of their life. That priority was putting Him first, also known as "have no other gods before me." They had allowed the work of the Lord to become more important than the

Lord of the work. The things that they were engaging in had taken the place of their relationship with Him.

How often have we seen ministers of the gospel get so involved with the work of the ministry that their relationship with God and their families suffer? They ultimately become ensnared with some kind of sinful behavior because their priorities are skewed. That can all be avoided if we will just remember our first love which is our first priority: put Jesus first.

Keeping First Things First

The Greek word that is translated "first" is *protos*. It means: foremost in time, place, order, or importance. Jesus was saying to the church at Ephesus that they had lost what should have been the most important thing within their lives. There was misplaced order within their priorities. The Lord was no longer first place in their lives. They had become distracted by good things that were keeping them from what was most important.

Think about this: your involvement in the kingdom of God started with a relationship with Jesus. That was the FIRST thing that took place. Your participation in the things of God FIRST began when you made Jesus Lord of your life. We come into the kingdom of God by FIRST making Him Lord, and the Lord must continue to be FIRST if we want to continue in His kingdom successfully. We must continue to place Him FIRST within our lives since that is where it all started.

There is a three-fold solution that Jesus gives for this issue of wrong priorities. He says to remember, repent, and do the first works. Remember where it all started. Repent by turning around and walking differently. Do the first works by stirring up the passion you once had for Him and His presence.

If you have fallen into this snare, I would encourage you to take the prescription of the Lord. Remember, repent, and do the FIRST works. Reignite your love and passion for Him. Fall in love with Jesus once again. Have no other gods before Him.

Practical Ways to Keep Him First

Let me give you some practical ways to keep the Lord first within your life. I believe that God makes things simple; He is not complicated. He does not make things difficult for us. So, these principles are simplistic in nature.

First of all is the principle of daily communion. Spend some time every day in prayer and worship. Do this at the beginning (first) of your day. Don't give God that which you have left over. Making Him first means giving Him your first. The Psalmist said, "Early will I seek you" (Psalm 63:1). Open up your Bible and hear what He has to say to you. Conduct a dialogue with the Lord, rather than a monologue.

Secondly is the principle of going to church. I know that might be a radical concept to some people, but you must understand that you can't love God without loving His church. The Apostle John said that if a man says he loves God and hates his brother (the church), he is a liar (1 John 4:20). To put Jesus first and love Him more than anything else, you must love His people.

Being in an environment where your faith and love for the Lord can be stirred regularly will help foster a vibrant relationship with God. Don't make excuses for yourself as to why you fail to attend church. The early church met on the FIRST day of the week. You need to put Him first by giving Him the FIRST day of your week.

The **third** principle for making Jesus first within your life is the principle of giving. Proverbs 3:9 declares that we are to honor the Lord with the FIRST-fruits of all of our increase. Again, we don't give to the Lord that which we have left over. We give to Him FIRST. He is the priority of our lives. Houses, cars, entertainment, clothing and anything else you can think of are not the priorities of our lives. The FIRST place we are to put our money is in the kingdom of God. Jesus is the priority of our lives.

As we put the Lord first, He will shower us with His blessings. Things will be added to us. Increase will be visible within our lives. As we make Him the priority of our lives, we will see great things take place. We are to seek first the kingdom of God. We are to put Jesus first within our lives; we are to have no other gods before Him.

Please pray this prayer with me:

Father God, I make a fresh commitment today to follow Your command to have no other gods before You. I appropriate forgiveness for any place within my life where I have broken this command. I receive deliverance and healing as I renounce the hidden works of darkness.

Today, I choose to obey Your command and put You first within my life. I will not allow anything or anyone else to take priority in my life from this day forward. You are the priority of my life. Thank You for Your grace that empowers and enables me to fulfill Your commandment. Thank You, Holy Spirit, for Your ability to live above sin. Sin will not have dominion over me. In the name of Jesus, I pray. Amen.

CHAPTER FOUR
THE MANDATE OF WORSHIP

"You shall not make for yourself a carved image—any likeness of anything that is in heaven above, or that is in the earth beneath, or that is in the water under the earth; you shall not bow down to them nor serve them. For I, the LORD your God, am a jealous God, visiting the iniquity of the fathers upon the children to the third and fourth generations of those who hate Me, but showing mercy to thousands, to those who love Me and keep My commandments" (Exodus 20:4-6).

We have seen that in the Old Covenant, God wrote upon tablets of stone. Now He writes on the tablet of our heart. What was carved upon an inanimate object is now carved within the fleshly heart of a living man. We are now the living carriers of the covenant of God within the earth.

As Christians, we have also seen that the grace of God does not separate us from commandments that are rearticulated in the New Testament. All of the Ten Commandments are still relevant for us today. Grace empowers us to now fulfill them from a heart of obedience.

We have seen how that Jesus, not only teaches us to obey the commandments, but actually takes them to the next level. He expounds on the heart of the commandments and deals with the root issues within the heart of mankind. Jesus further explains the heart of the Father within the commandments.

Now let's look at the next commandment given. The second commandment states that we are not to make any idols, bow down to them, nor serve them. This commandment deals with the subject of idolatry. It is strictly forbidden because God declares He is a jealous God.

There are specific consequences and blessings that God establishes in connection to this commandment. He declares that the consequence will be reaped within future generations. He also declares the blessing of obedience will be mercy to those who love Him and keep His commandments.

Forbidden in the Old and New Testament

We must first understand that just as idolatry is forbidden in the Old Testament, it is forbidden in the New. Nothing changed from the Old to the New. Grace does not say, "Now it's ok if you bow down to idols."

The Apostle Paul talks about idolatry as being the work of the flesh (Galatians 5:20). He goes on to say that "those who do such things will not inherit the kingdom of God" (Galatians 5:21). In other words, the people who practice idolatry will not experience the rule and reign of God within their lives. Simply put, the devil will rule within their lives. Wow!

This doesn't sound to me as if the second commandment has been removed or has become irrelevant. It appears to me that Paul is reemphasizing once again this important commandment of NO IDOLS! Idolatry is sin. Just as God said at the time of the giving of the commandment, Paul is reemphasizing the consequence of disobedience.

Penalty for Practice

Therefore put to death your members which are on the earth: fornication, uncleanness, passion, evil desire, and covetousness, which is idolatry. Because of these things the wrath of God is coming upon the sons of disobedience (Colossians 3:5-6).

Notice what Paul says immediately after the word idolatry: "Because of these things the wrath of God is coming on the sons of disobedience." I want to remind you that this is in the New Testament. Paul is saying God's wrath is going to be reaped in the lives of those who practice idolatry. It's coming upon them because they are sons of disobedience.

I recognize that this is not a popular subject preached in the pulpits of America, but you cannot continue to disobey God and expect to live free from consequence. Grace does not excuse unholy behavior as we have stated previously. God is very clear in both the Old Testament and New Testament that you cannot live a lifestyle of rebellion and experience the blessing of God at the same time. That would violate every spiritual principle that He has ever established.

In the post-modern church today, if a pastor was to get up and begin to preach the wrath of God is coming upon those who live in disobedience, he would be labeled a hate-monger and a minister of condemnation. It's amazing how much of the Bible we have conveniently ignored. It's astonishing how that the opinions of man along with social acceptance shape the sermons of many today.

It is not my intention to be critical, but rather bring to light how many who occupy the pulpits today have helped foster a culture in the church that ignores the consequences of disobedience in the name of grace and love. We have diminished many Scriptures that speak of the results of sin and embellished ones that speak only of forgiveness. This has resulted in an imbalance in the understanding of who God is, how He works with man, and what His expectation is concerning us who call ourselves Christians.

Once again, in this previous passage, the Apostle Paul in essence says to the church, "No idols." Was Paul preaching bondage in saying, "Put to death idolatry?" Absolutely not! He reinforced a commandment that is still relevant for us today.

I can hear some people saying, "Well, I don't have an idol that I bow down to." And may I reply to that, "Wonderful." However, anything that takes preeminence in our hearts above the Lord is an idol. Anything that we prefer above Him becomes something to which we are bowing. If there's anything within your life that has a higher place than Him, get rid of it!

Idolatry and Worship

Understand that people construct idols as representatives of a god that they worship. There are many different ways that these false gods are worshiped upon which we will not expound. However, bowing down to an idol was a common way in which those who practiced idolatry would worship. Bowing was a physical posture taken that indicated submission, honor, and allegiance. Thus, God forbids the making of a graven image for the purpose of bowing down to it in worship.

I want you to focus on the word "worship." Idols were a physical expression of a false god that people would worship. The purpose for the graven image was to give those worshiping

41

something to focus on. An idol was not a mere sculpted item or image, but rather something on which to focus.

Those who practiced idolatry would worship these idols expecting to receive something. They would do many different pagan acts within their worship of these idols to invoke various things. Idol worship involved witchcraft and would conjure demonic activity. We see this type of activity when Elijah had the showdown with the prophets of Baal.

Again, this was not merely a sculpted item. It was something used in false worship. The Apostle Paul said, "We know an idol is nothing" (1 Cor. 8:4). The idol itself is something that is made by man that has no power within itself. So, the problem was not so much the carving or creation of an inanimate object; the issue was that of worship.

The Heart of the Commandment

We see that God expressly said in the second commandment that His people were not to "bow down" to an idol. The Hebrew word used here for "bow down" is *shachah*. This word is translated in the book of Psalms on many occasions as the word *WORSHIP*. So the heart of the second commandment is really all about worship. It's not about an image; it's about worship.

We have to understand that even the Ark of the Covenant had cherubim made of gold on top of it. So, God was not declaring that there could be no works of art. He was not declaring there could be no paintings or carvings. The issue is WORSHIP.

Now let's look at what Jesus said:

Again, the devil took Him up on an exceedingly high mountain, and showed Him all the kingdoms of the world and their glory. And he said to Him, "All these things I will give You if You will fall down and worship me." Then Jesus said to him, "Away with you, Satan! For it is written, 'YOU SHALL WORSHIP THE LORD YOUR GOD, AND HIM ONLY YOU SHALL SERVE'" (Matthew 4:8-10).

In this passage of Scripture, we see the devil tempting the Lord to break the second commandment. Satan wanted Jesus to bow down and worship him. Many theologians believe that Jesus quoted a Scripture that is actually found in Deuteronomy 6:13, although the words are not exact. Let's read this passage in its entirety and see if it resembles one that we have read previously.

You shall fear (worship) the LORD your God and serve Him, and shall take oaths in His name. You shall not go after other gods, the gods of the peoples who are all around you (for the LORD your God is a jealous God among you), lest the anger of the LORD your God be aroused against you and destroy you from the face of the earth (Deuteronomy 6:13-15).

This sounds very similar to the second command contained in the Ten Commandments. The reason for this is that in the previous chapter, Moses rearticulates all of the Ten Commandments. In chapter six, where these verses are found, he is continuing to expound upon them. These verses are a restatement of the second commandment.

Isn't it interesting that when tempted by Satan to fall down and worship him, Jesus quoted a verse of Scripture that is actually the restatement of the second commandment. There are a lot of Scriptures that Jesus could have quoted that are scattered throughout the Old Testament. However, He chose one that has its basis in the second commandment.

Jesus stated the heart of the commandment when He declared, "You shall worship...Him only." He actually takes the second commandment to the next level. The commandment is more than just the abstinence of bowing down to an idol—it's about worshiping Jehovah God. This commandment is actually a mandate to worship God. Worship is a command, not an option! So, Jesus emphasizes the importance of worshiping God which is the fulfillment of the second commandment.

The reality is that every person will worship someone or something. The question is not if you will worship, but rather what or who you will worship. We all worship someone or something. God has commanded that we worship Him alone.

For every command there is a purpose. So what is the purpose for worship? Although there are many things that happen within our worship and as a result of worship, why does God command us to worship?

Think about this. In the first commandment we MAKE Him first. In the second commandment we KEEP Him first. Worship is a way in which we can keep Him first within our lives; it keeps Him upon the throne of our heart.

God's Original Intent

Understand that you were created to worship. Revelation 4:11 declares that God created all things for His pleasure. None of us were created to live for ourselves; we were created to live and worship Him. We were created to fulfill God's original design for our lives. Part of that design is to be a worshiper of Almighty God.

Understand that when we fail to worship Him, it is a perversion of God's original intent. God created man with a plan and intent in mind. That plan was perverted because of sin. However, Jesus came and regained everything that man lost at the fall.

When Adam was first created, God would come in the cool of the day and fellowship with Him. God would have communion with the man that He had created. I believe that Adam worshiped God during these times. We must understand that worship positions our heart for communion to take place. Adam could commune with God because he worshipped Him.

Worship Empowers

Let me share this principle with you: **that which you worship will be empowered within your life.** Worshiping God empowers His presence, glory, and grace within our lives. Anything or anyone that you hold in the highest esteem will be empowered within your life.

When anyone makes another person their idol (object of worship), like a movie star or music icon, anything their idol says becomes the absolute truth. Many times these idols can say illogical and ignorant things, and people will still repeat it and quote it.

You can see it in many of the lyrics of songs that the music idols sing. Lyrics can be unbiblical, filled with humanism, egotism, and arrogance and people will sing them repeatedly. Christians and unbelievers both do it.

I was in a public performance theater one day and noticed that before the performance there was music playing. As people filed in I noticed that many were singing the song that was playing over the PA. The words of the song exalted and praised human arrogance in that it said, "It's my life."

Well, Paul said it's not my life. He said my life is hid with Christ in God. He went on to say the life that I now live, I live by the faith of the Son of God. He said further that I am not my own, and I was bought with a price, that being the blood of Jesus. How dare I even say, "It's my life." That's a lie! My life belongs to Him!

I thought to myself this is the power of worship. When people worship someone (their music idol), they will sing anything that individual publishes. It can be filled with untruthful statements, profanity, anti-Christ statements and just about any other ungodly thing and people, both saved and unsaved, will repeat it.

I believe part of the reason God commands us to worship Him is that He wants us to repeat what He's saying! If we worship Him, we will start echoing that which heaven is declaring. If we worship Him, God will begin to speak to us in the midst of our worship. His Word will become what we sing and say.

The Power of Worship

Psalm 8:2 declares that our enemy is silenced when we worship God. I believe the opposite is equally true. Idolatry causes God to be silenced in one's life. The enemy's voice is amplified and God's voice is silenced through idolatry. Idolatry empowers the enemy, but true worship empowers God. Who do you want to be empowered in your life? I want the Lord empowered so I'm going to worship Him.

I wrote a book many years ago on the power of praise and worship as a weapon of spiritual warfare. The previous Scripture I referred to actually says that God has ordained praise because of our enemy. It goes on to say that praise causes the enemy to fail. Can you see why the enemy wants us to cease worshiping God? Our worship is that which God has ordained to cause Satan's plans to fail and falter. Satan's defense is to have people participate in a lifestyle of idolatry since it keeps them from worshipping God. It also strengthens his hold on the people who commit such acts.

If you ask most Christians the question of what they are going to do when they get to heaven, they will answer by saying, "Worship the Lord." I believe that is true. We will worship God. However, I believe that the second commandment infers that you can't worship in heaven until you do it on earth. Think about it.

The Heart of Worship and Vain Worship

It is important to understand that worship begins in the heart. The outward expression of worship should be indicative of what is already taking place on the inside. Worship should signify a submitted heart to the Lord. It should indicate that there is a bowing down of our will and total surrender to Him. If we are going through motions of worship without a heart of worship, we participate in vain worship.

Jesus speaking of the Pharisees said, "In vain they worship me" (Matthew 15:9). The Pharisees went through the motions of worship, but their hearts were far from the Lord. The interesting thing about the place where Jesus talks about the vain worship of the Pharisees is in conjunction with Him discussing one of the Ten Commandments. He was speaking specifically of the fifth commandment that says to honor your father and mother. Let's read it.

> He answered and said to them, "Why do you also transgress the commandment of God because of your tradition? For God commanded, saying, 'HONOR YOUR FATHER AND YOUR MOTHER;' and, 'HE WHO CURSES FATHER OR MOTHER, LET HIM BE PUT TO DEATH.' But you say, 'Whoever says to his father or mother, "Whatever profit you might have received from me is a gift to God"—then he need not honor his father or mother.' Thus you have made the commandment of God of no effect by your tradition. Hypocrites! Well did Isaiah prophesy about you, saying: 'THESE PEOPLE DRAW NEAR TO ME WITH THEIR MOUTH, AND HONOR ME WITH THEIR LIPS,

BUT THEIR HEART IS FAR FROM ME. AND IN VAIN THEY WORSHIP ME, TEACHING AS DOCTRINES THE COMMANDMENTS OF MEN'" (Matthew 15:3-9).

The Pharisees had created a way that you could "opt out" of the commandment. It is similar to the way that some have used grace as a means to "opt out" of other commandments. They had made a way that through the giving of a gift one could be excused from obeying the command of honoring their parents. Jesus rebuked them sharply saying that they had made the commandment of no effect because they had substituted it with a tradition created by man.

Could it be that ignoring the commandments produces vain worship? Could it be that we can sing, lift our hands, and shout and it be worthless to the Lord? Could it be that changing or watering down what God has repeatedly commanded will cause our acts of worship to be meaningless? Selah.

The problem with the Pharisees is a contemporary issue. It is the reasoning of man in an attempt to justify behavior that is lawless. It is the exalting of man's idea over the commands that God has specifically given. It is a rationale that minimizes clear directives that God has given and maximizes that which is more palatable to the flesh and yet still appears spiritual.

It is time for believers to rise up and reject this kind of thinking. If we want our worship to be effective, we must walk in obedience. If we want God's promise empowered within our lives, we must choose His command over the doctrines of men.

We must remember that worship begins with the heart. At the heart of the second commandment is the mandate of worship. It's not a suggestion, it's a commandment. I encourage you to obey and worship Him with all of your being.

Please pray this prayer with me:

Father God, I make a fresh commitment today to follow Your command to worship no one but You. I appropriate forgiveness for any place within my life where I have broken this command. I receive deliverance and healing as I renounce the hidden works of darkness.

Today, I forsake any and all types of manifestations of idolatry. I choose to worship You, Lord. I choose to live my life as a worshipper of You, rather than an idolater. Thank You for Your grace that empowers and enables me to fulfill Your commandment. Thank You, Holy Spirit, for Your ability to live above sin. Sin will not have dominion over me. In the name of Jesus, I pray. Amen.

CHAPTER FIVE
HONORING THE NAME

*"You shall not take the name of the LORD
your God in vain, for the LORD will not hold
him guiltless who takes His name in vain"
(Exodus 20:7).*

Here we see the third commandment that is given. We are not to take the Lord's name in vain. The command goes on to say that God will hold the person who does such a thing responsible for his actions. Obviously, this is conduct in which none of us as Christians should be engaging.

So, exactly what does this mean? We have been traditionally taught that using the Lord's name in vain is using the Lord's name in conjunction with profanity. By doing so, we profane the name of the Lord. Using the name of the Lord in a way that we call "cussing" or "cursing" should not be practiced by believers. Using the name of Jesus in a flippant or irreverent manner is biblically forbidden.

To have a greater understanding of this, we need to define the word "vain." It means desolating, evil, useless, and destructive. So, God is commanding that His name not be used in an inappropriate manner. It is not to be used in a useless and evil manner. It is not to be used in a desolating or destructive manner. However, it is to be used in a correct manner.

I believe the best way to keep from misusing or abusing something is to treat it correctly. The best way to keep from using something improperly is to use it properly. The best way to keep from taking the Lord's name in vain is to use it in the way Jesus commanded us.

Once again, we are getting to the heart of the commandment. This is not merely a commandment that forbids using the name of the Lord with profane expletives. It is an exhortation to use the name of the Lord in the manner that it was intended!

This command in the affirmative is a directive to honor the name of the Lord. We are to understand the power that the Father has invested within the name of Jesus. It is a command to give the name of the Lord its proper and rightful place. We are to place the name of the Lord in the greatest position and place as we recognize that His name is higher than any other.

Jesus Reinforces the Commandment

"In this manner, therefore, pray: Our Father in heaven, Hallowed be Your name" (Matthew 6:9).

Jesus actually reinforces the third commandment in this Scripture. He teaches His disciples to pray that the name of the Lord be hallowed. The word "hallowed" means holy, pure, and consecrated. So, Jesus teaches His disciples that the name of the Lord is not to be taken in vain; it is to be kept holy, pure, and consecrated.

It's very interesting reading Matthew 6:9 in different translations. Let me share just a few of them in order to give a fuller understanding:

"You should pray like this: Our Father in heaven, help us to honor your name" (CEV).

"So this is how you should pray: 'Our Father in heaven, we pray that your name will always be kept holy'" (ERV).

"This, then, is how you should pray: 'Our Father in heaven: May your holy name be honored'" (GNB).

Are you getting the picture? Jesus is articulating the heart of the third commandment. The heart of it is to honor the name of the Lord. Keep His name holy. The name of the Lord is to be reserved for that which it is intended and not to be profaned. We will discuss later the proper uses of the name of the Lord.

> *Therefore God also has highly exalted Him and given Him the name which is above every name, that at the name of Jesus every knee should bow, of those in heaven, and of those on earth, and of those under the earth, and that every tongue should confess that Jesus Christ is Lord, to the glory of God the Father (Philippians 2:9-11).*

Jesus has been given a name that is above every name. His name is higher than any other. His name is not to be used flippantly or irreverently. His name is to be exalted and worshiped. His name is to be revered.

I believe that all Christians today have somewhat of an understanding of this principle. However, there are many today who do not have a full grasp of everything which that entails.

When you read the above passage of Scripture, it starts with the word "therefore." When you see the word "therefore," you should see what it is "there for."

Looking back at the preceding verse, we see why Jesus was exalted and given a name that is above every other.

Obedience and Honor

"And being found in appearance as a man, He humbled Himself and became obedient to the point of death, even the death of the cross" (Philippians 2:8).

Notice what Jesus did: He humbled Himself and became OBEDIENT to the point of death. Jesus was submitted to the will of the Father to the degree that He was willing to die. Jesus obeyed the Father and in doing so was then exalted and given a name above every other.

You are probably asking, "What does that have to do with honoring the name of the Lord?" I'm glad you asked.

To honor the name of the Lord that was given because of obedience means that obedience must be reciprocated in order to honor His name. The greatest way we honor and revere the name of the Lord is through a lifestyle of obedience to Him. Jesus Himself said, "Why do you call me 'Lord, Lord,' and not do the things that I say?" (Luke 6:46).

Jesus is declaring that honoring Him begins with obedience. Let me say it another way. Disobedience to God dishonors His name. We who are called Christians, who name the name of Jesus, should live up to that name. We should not do anything to bring reproach on His name. If we do, we have taken the name of the Lord in vain.

New Programming Is Needed

I understand that all of us at some time or another have disobeyed the Lord and His Word. I recognize that we all have failed. There are various reasons that all of us could give. One reason for failure is because we have been taught that we will most certainly fail. We have been programmed to sin through teaching that emphasizes fleshly weakness. Our minds have been programmed with "I will fail" rather than "He is able to keep me from falling" (Jude 1:24).

I am so thankful for the revelation of God's grace. You cannot get too much of it. We all need a greater revelation of His grace which is sufficient. But understand His grace is not just for forgiveness, it is for empowerment. His grace enables us to obey. His grace empowers us to live above sin and disobedience.

As a parent, one of the greatest ways that my child can dishonor me is to disobey. No parent is proud of their children when they commit a crime. No parent wants to produce an advertisement in the morning paper of how their child has been sentenced to twenty years for armed robbery. Their child's actions have dishonored their name.

This in no way means that parents cease to love their children. It means that needless embarrassment has been brought to the parents as a result of their child's behavior. Likewise, we dishonor the name of the Lord when we conduct our lives in a rebellious manner and disobey His Word.

Jesus has been given a name that is highly exalted. We as Christians are wearing that name. How are we representing Him? Are we bringing honor to the name of the Lord? Are our actions giving glory to the name of Jesus or bringing shame?

Please understand that I am in no way condemning anyone. However, I do want us to realize that grace does not excuse sin or the breaking of God's commandments given. We need to begin to rely on the grace of God in the way of empowering us to do what is pleasing in His sight.

Unauthorized Use Is Vain Use

Now God worked unusual miracles by the hands of Paul, so that even handkerchiefs or aprons were brought from his body to the sick, and the diseases left them and the evil spirits went out of them. Then some of the itinerant Jewish exorcists took it upon themselves to call the name of the Lord Jesus over those who had evil spirits, saying, "We exorcise you by the Jesus whom Paul preaches." Also there were seven sons of Sceva, a Jewish chief priest, who did so. And the evil spirit answered and said, "Jesus I know, and Paul I know; but who are you?" Then the man in whom the evil spirit was leaped on them, overpowered them, and prevailed against them, so that they fled out of that house naked and wounded. This became known both to all Jews and Greeks dwelling in Ephesus; and fear fell on them all, and the name of the Lord Jesus was magnified (Acts 19:11-17).

You can only use a name if you have been authorized to do so. Invoking another person's name in an unauthorized manner is actually a crime. It is called identity theft. If one were to take your personal information and use it to open up a line of credit, one would be committing fraud, and they would go to prison for such a crime.

In the above passage of Scripture, we see an unauthorized use of the name of the Lord. These sons of Sceva were not saved; they were not Christians. They had not been washed in the blood of Jesus. However, they attempted to mimic that which they had seen and heard Paul do. The result was not good.

Notice what the sons of Sceva said, "We exorcise (cast you out) by the Jesus whom Paul preaches." Hearing Paul preach the name of Jesus did not authorize them to use the name of Jesus. Witnessing Paul cast out devils did not empower them to do so.

These men were taking the name of the Lord in vain. They were using the name of Jesus like a lucky rabbit's foot. They saw it as a formula to produce results with no relationship with the One whose name they were using. These men were idiots. However, we can learn from their grave mistake.

Then the demonic spirit within this man said, "I know Jesus, and I know Paul, but who are you?" (author's paraphrase). The demon recognized that the sons of Sceva were not authorized to use the name because they were not saved. You can't use the family name if you don't belong to the family. Becoming a part of the family of God is that which entitles you to use the name of Jesus.

Honor and Identify

I personally believe that the reason the demon said, "Jesus I know, and Paul I know," was because honoring the name of the Lord is what identifies you with it. These sons of Sceva had not honored the name of Jesus. They had never exercised faith in the name to receive salvation. They had not called upon the name of the Lord. They had never identified themselves with the name of Jesus.

This demon spirit knew Paul because Paul knew Jesus. Paul identified himself with the Lord as he honored the name of Jesus. Honoring and revering the name of Jesus is what identifies us with Him.

The good news for us who have believed on Him is that the name of Jesus has all authority and power. It authorizes you to do and empowers you to perform. The name of Jesus is higher than any other and will be honored as we use His name to bring glory to God.

As was stated previously, the heart of the third commandment is articulated again in the New Testament. It is a command that grace does not take away or diminish. Grace actually takes it to a higher level and requirement.

In the Old Testament you could not take the name of the Lord in vain. In the New Testament you are to bring honor to His name by using it properly. It is to be revered and kept holy. We are to use the name of Jesus in ways that bring glory and honor to the Lord since His name has been delegated to us. We are responsible to see this done.

Let me quickly give you some ways that we honor the name of the Lord and in doing so fulfill the third commandment.

BELIEVE on the Name of the Lord

The fulfillment of the third commandment starts by BELIEVING in His name. Place your trust and confidence in the name of the Lord. The Psalmist said, "Some trust in chariots, some in horses, but we will remember the name of the Lord our God" (Psalm 20:7). King Solomon said, "The name of the Lord is a strong tower, the righteous run to it and are safe" (Proverbs 18:10).

There is power in the name of Jesus. There is salvation in the name of Jesus. There is deliverance in the name of Jesus. There is healing in the name of Jesus. Why would we put our trust in anything or anyone else?

Then Peter said, "Silver and gold I do not have, but what I do have I give you: In the name of Jesus Christ of Nazareth, rise up and walk." And he took him by the right hand and lifted him up, and immediately his feet and ankle bones received strength. So he, leaping up, stood and walked and entered the temple with them— walking, leaping, and praising God. And all the people saw him walking and praising God. Then they knew that it was he who sat begging alms at the Beautiful Gate of the temple; and they were filled with wonder and amazement at what had happened to him. Now as the lame man who was healed held on to Peter and John, all the people ran together to them in the porch which is called Solomon's, greatly amazed. And His name, through faith in His name, has made this man strong, whom you see and know. Yes, the faith which comes through Him has given him this perfect sound-ness in the presence of you all (Acts 3:6-11, 16).

Here is a wonderful account of the name of Jesus being used properly. Remember that part of the definition for taking the name of the Lord in vain is "to consider useless." Here the name of Jesus is invoked in a useful manner. Peter used the name of Jesus to bring healing to a crippled man.

Jesus said to His disciples in Mark 16 that "these signs will follow them that BELIEVE in my name...they will lay hands on the sick and they will recover." I think it's interesting that Jesus points out that signs and miracles follow those who BE-LIEVE in His name. Believing in the name of Jesus authorizes you to use it. Believing in the power of that name will bring about miracles! Hallelujah!

Notice what Peter says in verse sixteen after everyone is marveling at this man's healing, "His name (the name of Jesus), through faith in His name, has made this man strong." Peter was actually saying that honoring the name of the Lord by be-lieving in it brought forth this man's healing. The name of Jesus receives glory when healing and miracles take place in His name!

I believe that God desires to be glorified. The crippled man was not giving God any glory by begging at the gate Beautiful. I'm sure he invoked a lot of pity, but not a lot of glory. But notice what happened once he received his healing in the name of Jesus. The Bible says that he began to walk, leap, and praise God. God started getting glory when he was healed! When the name of Jesus was honored, God received praise!

That brings us to the next principle for honoring the name of the Lord.

PRAISE the Name of the Lord

The word most commonly translated "praise" is the Hebrew word *halal*. It means to celebrate, boast and to be clamorously foolish. I tell people that you can't take the name of the Lord in vain while you *halal* Him.

Praising the name of the Lord is something in which we are all commanded. One of the reasons I believe that God has commanded this is to prevent us from taking His name in vain. When you praise the name of the Lord, you place it in a position of honor. When you exalt His name within your life, it takes a place of preeminence.

I have noticed that those who praise and worship the Lord regularly are not the ones heard using profanities. It's the ones who never praise the Lord that take His name in vain the most. It is the ones who don't glorify the name of the Lord that break God's commandments regularly. Could there be a connection? I think so.

As I stated in a previous chapter, that which you worship will be empowered within your life. The name of the Lord is empowered when you praise Him. If you want the name of the Lord to be honored in your life then start praising it!

There are numerous Psalms we read that contain direct commands to praise the name of the Lord. Repeatedly, we see David exhorting the people of God to worship, revere, honor, and praise the name of the Lord. Not only is it in the Old Testament, but it's in the New Testament also! Are you surprised?

Think about it. God didn't change from the Old to the New. Jesus is the same yesterday, today, and forever. His moral commands are still the same. Some may be articulated differently in the New Testament, but the spirit and heart of the commandments are the same.

"Therefore by Him let us continually offer the sacrifice of praise to God, that is, the fruit of our lips, giving thanks to His name" (Hebrews 13:15).

The writer of Hebrews says that the fruit of our lips is to be the giving of thanks to His name. The fruit of our lips can be that which glorifies the name of the Lord or that which takes His name in vain. The choice is ours.

Since that name is the name by which I was delivered from the kingdom of darkness, then I owe that name honor. Since that name is the name by which I received eternal life, then I owe that name reverence. Since that name is the name by which I received my healing, then I owe that name the highest place within my life. If you are saved, you owe the name of the Lord the highest praise!

Here is the next way we can honor the name of the Lord and fulfill His commandment.

REMEMBER the Name of the Lord

"Some trust in chariots, and some in horses; But we will remember the name of the LORD our God. They have bowed down and fallen; But we have risen and stand upright" (Psalm 20:7-8).

Once again, we are talking about the third command of the Ten Commandments. The command is that the name of the Lord is not to be taken in vain. It is not to be desecrated, defamed, misused, or taken improperly. This command carries over into the New Testament since we see both exhortations and demonstrations of proper use for the name of the Lord.

The Psalmist said, "We will remember the name of the Lord our God." The word "remember" used in this verse means mark so as to be recognized, to be mindful, mention, and recount. The Psalmist is saying we are to be mindful of the name of the Lord. We are to mention and speak out the name of the Lord. His name is to be recognized in all of its splendor and majesty.

The blessing of remembering the name of the Lord is that our enemy falls. And it doesn't stop there. He goes on to say that we will rise and stand upright. Here is the spiritual principle of reciprocation in operation. We exalt and lift up the name of the Lord and He causes us to be lifted up. He causes us to arise when we raise high His name. How awesome is that?

Understand that anytime we obey God there is a blessing that follows. In Deuteronomy 28, God articulates the blessings of obedience. He declares if we will diligently listen to the voice of the Lord and do all that He commands, blessings will come upon us and overtake us. God's blessings come as a result of obedience.

I think one thing that many people miss when they read the Old Testament is that God was usually speaking to the people with whom He had made covenant. Even though the children of Israel had a covenant with God that promised them deliverance, healing, and prosperity, the fulfillment of the promises was predicated on obedience. God's promises were conditional. God said if they would obey, then He would bless. However, He also said that if they disobeyed, they would be cursed.

I've known of people who go around quoting the verse in Galatians that declares we have been redeemed from the curse of the law while they live a lifestyle of sin. Then they scratch their heads trying to figure out why nothing is working out for them. It's easy to discern the problem; disobedience is the culprit. Their disobedience opens the door for the thief to come in and steal, kill, and destroy.

I want you to see an account where David remembered the name of the Lord:

> *Then David said to the Philistine, "You come to me with a sword, with a spear, and with a javelin. But I come to you in the name of the LORD of hosts, the God of the armies of Israel, whom you have defied. This day the LORD will deliver you into my hand, and I will strike you and take your head from you. And this day I will give the carcasses of the camp of the Philistines to the birds of the air and the wild beasts of the earth, that all the earth may know that there is a God in Israel" (1 Samuel 17:45-46).*

Part of remembering the name of the Lord is recalling the victories that you have seen within your life. Before David went out to meet Goliath, he had to deal with King Saul. Saul tried to dissuade David from fighting Goliath. Saul told him he was just a boy while exalting all of Goliath's attributes.

With friends like that you don't need any enemies. I'm actually convinced that David's mental and psychological battle with condescending and critical comments was greater than the one with Goliath. He had to wade through the discouraging words of his brother and then King Saul. No one was excited about David's prospects.

However, David had a key that others didn't. He REMEMBERED the name of the Lord. He started recalling and rehearsing his previous victories. He told Saul that he had faced a lion and a bear, killed both of them, and gave credit to the Lord (the name of the Lord) for the accomplishment. He went on to say, "The Lord who delivered me from the paw of the lion and the paw of the bear will deliver me from the hand of this Philistine!"

Saul then wanted to suit David up in his armor. David said "thanks, but no thanks." I personally believe that Saul wanted David to wear his armor so he could get some credit if David were to win. My question has always been if Saul's armor was so great, why didn't he go fight Goliath wearing it? David recognized that armor would not cause him to gain the victory. It was the name of the Lord that would be the determining factor. The name of the Lord worked when he faced the lion and the bear, and he believed that it would work against Goliath.

David gathered five smooth stones and a sling. Then he went out to meet the giant and started prophesying to him. He declared to Goliath, "I come to you in the name of the LORD of hosts, the God of the armies of Israel, whom you have defied."

Notice that David said Goliath had defied the name of the Lord. Some translations declare that Goliath insulted the name of the Lord. The Hebrew word for "defied" means defame or blaspheme. Goliath had cursed the name of the Lord. One translation of this account declares that Goliath used the names of his gods to say curses against David (ESV).

Get a picture of what's happening here. It is name against name. It is the name of Goliath's gods against the name of the Lord. It is a showdown of whose name would be the most powerful.

The rest of the story is a very familiar one. David killed Goliath. Those who take the name of the Lord in vain don't last long enough to brag about it. Those who use the name of the Lord in the proper manner see victory and triumph. David triumphed over the giant because he honored and reverenced the name of the Lord. Goliath was beheaded because he took the name of the Lord in vain.

David remembered the name of the Lord. He honored the name of the Lord as he triumphed over Goliath. David used the name of the Lord in a manner that brought glory.

Your giant will fall just like Goliath as you remember the name of the Lord. Honor the name of the Lord today and see your enemy fall. You will be like David who said, "They have bowed down and fallen; but we have risen and stand upright" (Psalm 20:8).

Please pray this prayer with me:

Father God, I make a fresh commitment today to follow Your command to not take Your name in vain. I appropriate forgiveness for any place within my life where I have broken this command. I receive deliverance and healing as I renounce the hidden works of darkness.

Today, I forsake any and all types of foul speech and anything that would dishonor Your name. I choose to use Your name correctly and honorably. I choose to believe in Your name, praise Your name, and remember Your name. Thank You for Your grace that empowers and enables me to fulfill Your commandment. Thank You, Holy Spirit, for Your ability to live above sin. Sin will not have dominion over me. In the name of Jesus, I pray. Amen.

CHAPTER SIX
GET PLANTED

"Remember the Sabbath day, to keep it holy. Six days you shall labor and do all your work, but the seventh day is the Sabbath of the LORD your God. In it you shall do no work: you, nor your son, nor your daughter, nor your male servant, nor your female servant, nor your cattle, nor your stranger who is within your gates. For in six days the LORD made the heavens and the earth, the sea, and all that is in them, and rested the seventh day. Therefore the LORD blessed the Sabbath day and hallowed it" (Exodus 20:8-11).

Here we see God initiating the fourth commandment. God commanded His people to remember the Sabbath Day; they were to observe a day of rest. They were to take a pause during the week for three primary reasons. The reasons were REST, REFRESHING, and RECIPROCATION. We will talk more in detail on these later.

With each of the Ten Commandments there are underlying spiritual principles that govern them. It is needful for us to understand the heart of the Father within each of the commandments that He gave. As we hear God's heart on the matter, there is a positive motivation that will arise within our hearts.

The underlying principle of this commandment is for God's people to GET PLANTED AND GO TO CHURCH.

The Origins of the Sabbath

Let's first of all determine exactly where the Sabbath originated. Some would try to argue that the Sabbath began with the introduction of the Law, but that is not accurate.

> *And on the seventh day God ended His work which He had done, and He rested on the seventh day from all His work which He had done. Then God blessed the seventh day and sanctified it, because in it He rested from all His work which God had created and made (Genesis 2:2-3).*

As you read this passage of Scripture, it can clearly be seen that the Sabbath originated at the time of creation. It did not originate at the time of the giving of the Law.

Sabbath means to desist from exertion; speaking more specifically of labor and toil. At the time of creation, God paused to take a break on the seventh day. He ceased from His labor in order to rest and be refreshed.

In doing so, God left a pattern that we were to follow throughout the days of our existence here on earth. This was not something that was done with no forethought or spiritual significance. God deliberately instituted a day of rest in order to show by example what you and I should take part in today. At a later time, when the Law was given, God made it a commandment.

When God said for His people to "remember the Sabbath Day," He literally meant **to remember**. The word "remember" means to recall. God gave an instruction to His covenant people to bring to the forefront of their thinking that which He instituted at creation. The commandment that He was giving was not something new. It was a principle that was already in operation before the Law was given.

A Holy Convocation

"Six days shall work be done, but the seventh day is a Sabbath of solemn rest, a holy convocation" (Leviticus 23:3).

God commanded His covenant people to set the seventh day apart and consecrate it for His kingdom purpose. The Sabbath was designed by Almighty God at the time of creation to be an opportunity for man to be refreshed both naturally and spiritually. It was designed to be a day where those of like precious faith congregated together for His divine purpose.

The word **convocation** means a public meeting. This Hebrew word is translated *assemblies* on several occasions. The Sabbath was to be a day set apart for the people of God to meet publicly at a certain place of assembly. GOD DESIGNED IT THAT WAY! This was not my plan, nor am I saying this only because I am a pastor. This was and is God's design.

There are some who have accused church pastors of only being interested in the growth of their local churches. They feel that the exhortation of being in the house of the Lord is meant only to provide the pastor with someone whom to minister. First of all, let me respond to that false assumption by saying that pastors have the God-given responsibility to preach and teach the Word of God which includes the commandment of believers gathering together and being in the house of the Lord.

We must understand that pastors have been delegated a business which is to teach, preach, and proclaim that which God's Word says and motivate those who have ears to hear and obey. Pastors should tell their congregation members of their God-given responsibility to the local church.

There are yet others who feel that the commandment to keep the Sabbath Day holy is an outdated commandment that does not fit with the current trends of our culture. They say that the pace of life today does not allow for the fulfilling of this commandment. They go on to declare that it is impossible for them to honor the Lord in this manner because of other responsibilities of life. I will attempt to address each one of these as best I can.

God Does Not Change

We must first realize that God's Word does not change according to the current trends of our culture. God's Word is forever settled in heaven. If you begin going down that path, you are headed for danger. It leads to a life philosophy called situational ethics that determines right and wrong behavior only by the circumstance that one encounters.

It is a lie from the enemy that causes people, including believers, to take a path that leads to all manner of sin and self-destruction. If we relegate the Word of God to its interpretation in light of cultural trends at a given moment, we are guilty of the sin of Balaam. He compromised his integrity by opening the door of temptation and coveting money and acceptance.

Another realization that must be had is that our pace of life should be determined by God's command and not our external desires and influences. To say that our pace of life is too busy is to idolize our own endeavors. It places our "own thing" above "God's thing." By doing so, we have broken the first commandment which says, "You shall have no other gods before Me" (Exodus 20:3).

If we say our own business is in the way of us fulfilling God's commandment, then we have placed our own undertakings before the Lord. This is idolatry.

Natural Responsibilities and Obedience

I understand that we all have responsibilities. Life is filled with them. It is good that we take responsibility for our lives and become productive individuals. God commands us to be productive and fruitful. However, the responsibilities of life are not intended to supersede the commandment of the Lord.

Jesus spoke of the person who allowed the cares of life to choke the Word. There are many believers who are allowing their responsibilities (cares of life) to choke out the Word to the point that they no longer obey what it says. The end result of this lifestyle is fruitlessness. We must not allow our "busy-ness" to keep us from fulfilling God's command of keeping the Sabbath Day holy.

On the other hand, God's command was never imposed for the purpose of burdening us with obligation nor putting us in bondage to the point of not being able to "lift a finger" on the Sabbath. Remember that there is a ditch on each side of the road. Let's see what Jesus had to say about the Sabbath.

Now it happened that He went through the grainfields on the Sabbath; and as they went His disciples began to pluck the heads of grain. And the Pharisees said to Him, "Look, why do they do what is not lawful on the Sabbath?" But He said to them, "Have you never read what David did when he was in need and hungry, he and those with him: how he went into the house of God in the days of Abiathar the high priest, and ate the showbread, which is not lawful to eat, except for the priests, and also gave some to those who were with him?" And He said to them, "The Sabbath was made

*for man, and not man for the Sabbath. Therefore the
Son of Man is also Lord of the Sabbath" (Mark 2:23-
28).*

The Ditch of Legalism

The Pharisees were always looking for something
whereby they could make accusations against Jesus. This was
very difficult for them since Jesus obeyed and followed the
commandments—one of them being to keep the Sabbath Day
holy. The Pharisees were those who were experts in matters
pertaining to Jewish legalism, but had little understanding as to
the purpose for the law itself. Being blinded by their own
bondage to legalism and lack of love, they seemed to miss the
heart of God.

In response to the accusation made by the Pharisees,
Jesus said, "The Sabbath was made for man, and not man for
the Sabbath." Jesus was articulating the purpose and spirit of
the law. He was telling them, 'You have missed the entire purpose for the Sabbath Day because you are bound by legalistic
opinions and interpretation of God's command. Do you not realize that picking corn for food has absolutely nothing to do
with honoring the Sabbath Day? Feeding myself does not violate the Sabbath because it was created so man could be fed
and refreshed.'

The "spiritual Bozos" of the day were upset about Jesus
being refreshed. They were so concerned about Jesus doing
something unlawful on the Sabbath that they failed to keep the
commandment of loving their neighbor as themselves. I do not
think they would have appreciated being spied on like they
were doing to Jesus.

When Jesus spoke to the Pharisees, He addressed their
incorrect interpretation of the commandment. They were
bound by the "letter of the law" and neglected the spirit and
heart of the commandment. This was a common problem with

the Pharisees; they were blinded by legalism. They couldn't see the forest for the trees. Jesus knew the Father's purpose for the commandment of remembering the Sabbath Day. It had already been articulated clearly in the Word of God.

> *"Therefore the children of Israel shall keep the Sabbath, to observe the Sabbath throughout their generations as a perpetual covenant. It is a sign between Me and the children of Israel forever; for in six days the LORD made the heavens and the earth, and on the seventh day He rested and was refreshed"* (Exodus 31:16-17).

The Ditch of No Observance

There are some today who have taken the account of Jesus' confrontation of the Pharisees concerning the Sabbath Day and made a doctrine that it no longer matters if you set aside a day to honor the Lord or if you don't. The argument that is made claims Jesus abolished the observance of the Sabbath Day by precept, example, and in His sacrificial offering. I assure you, my friend, nothing could be further from the truth.

The first thing we must understand is that Jesus did observe the Sabbath. He frequented the Synagogue on a regular (weekly) basis. By His example, Jesus upheld the fourth commandment and He kept the Sabbath Day holy unto the Lord. It was a habit He had developed since His birth.

"So He came to Nazareth, where He had been brought up. And as His custom was, He went into the synagogue on the Sabbath day, and stood up to read" (Luke 4:16).

The Example of Jesus

The example Jesus left for you and me to follow was to go to church on a weekly basis. He exemplified honoring the

Lord on the Sabbath Day. Everything that Jesus taught and demonstrated upheld the principle and commandment of keeping the Sabbath Day holy unto the Lord.

If Jesus had wanted to abolish this commandment then He would have said so in an unambiguous fashion. He had an opportunity to do so when He responded to the accusation of the Pharisees against Him, but did not. He only restated the commandment with a clearer understanding of God's divine purpose. That certainly does not classify as an abolishing of this important commandment.

Jesus went to church on a weekly basis. We do not have His attendance records with us today, but we do have the words of the Bible that declare it was His custom to go to the synagogue on the Sabbath Day. Jesus was a faithful member of His local assembly. If we are to follow the example of Jesus, then we will remember the Sabbath Day.

Jesus had an understanding of the Law, but His obedience was not born out of a mere adherence to a code of conduct. He had an understanding of the heart of the Father as to why the commandment was there in the first place. Jesus never said he abhorred the commandments in their purest form. Rather, He confronted the religious traditions of men that discredited and dishonored the commandments that the Father had given to mankind.

When Jesus laid down His life to pay the price for our redemption and make a way for God's grace to be extended to all of mankind, there is no scriptural indication that the Ten Commandments were abolished. There were some things that were done away with, but the Ten Commandments were not. Hence, the commandment of keeping the Sabbath Day holy remains relevant for those in the New Covenant.

Controversy Concerning the Commandments

There has been great controversy concerning the Ten Commandments in days past. In one incident, a monument of the Ten Commandments was removed from a public building. Christians were appalled and angry—me being one of them. It was unthinkable that in the United States of America something of this magnitude could happen.

As I was watching some of the news coverage of this on television, the thought came to me that many Christians took greater offense over the monument being removed from a building than the breaking and dishonoring of the Commandments. I am not saying that we should not be outraged about this kind of judicial tyranny. However, if we are going to be infuriated about the removal of a monument of the Ten Commandments, we should certainly be following and obeying them.

Again, it deserves to be repeated that the Sabbath Day originated at the time of creation, not the Law. It is a divine principle that the Father initiated at the beginning of time as we know it. It is more than a commandment, law, or regulation; it is a statute that was instituted the day following the creation of man.

In the writings of the Apostle Paul, he restates many of the Ten Commandments. Paul would not reaffirm any of these if they were not relevant for believers in the New Testament. Not only did Paul articulate these commandments, but he also practiced all of them including keeping the Sabbath Day holy.

"And he reasoned in the synagogue every Sabbath" (Acts 18:4).

Notice it didn't say *some* Sabbaths, but rather *every* Sabbath. Paul was committed to obeying the Ten Commandments. Paul was committed to honoring the Lord by honoring the Sabbath Day. He knew the Sabbath was intended for the convocation of believers so he went to church.

Excuses, Circumstances, and Justifications

It amazes me today how some believers are so easily removed from a place of obedience by some of the smallest and minute circumstances. If Junior has a hang nail, then it is a good enough reason for them to not go to the house of the Lord. The latest episode of their favorite Sunday sitcom is much more important than a church service. After all, they would "absolutely die" if they missed their favorite television show. What are our priorities? Where is the heart of obedience and commitment?

Some have used the word "grace" to excuse the non-adherence to any commandment that may restrict their behavior. We have heard things such as, "If your conscience does not bother you, then it's OK." While I will concede there are some things God has left for matters of personal conviction, when a conscience is seared any action becomes approved. Even the disobedience of clearly articulated commandments is tolerated when your conscience no longer troubles you. Anyone who gets to this place will be led by the enemy into a place of captivity.

Grace Does Not Excuse but Rather Empowers

Grace does not excuse anyone from obeying the Bible. It is quite the contrary. Grace enables us to obey and fulfill what God has told us to do. Grace gives us the ability to obey from our hearts with the understanding of God's divine purpose. Grace is what has now caused His commandments to be written upon the tablets of our hearts. We are not merely adhering to a code of conduct that has been prescribed and forced upon us. We are the sons and daughters of God who take delight in obeying His commands.

Grace is what gives us power to overcome sin and self-will. Grace empowers us to fulfill the call of God upon our lives. Grace is not and never will be an excuse to participate in fleshly and sinful behavior. Neither will it ever legitimize the annulment of God's commandments in the lives of believers.

The Commandments Are Still Relevant

When Jesus died at Calvary, the Bible declares that He removed the handwriting of ordinances that were against us as they were nailed to the cross in Him (Colossians 2:14). The Apostle Paul wrote this to the Colossians. Some have interpreted this to say that all commandments that were in the Old Testament have been negated, and they are not applicable to those living under the New Covenant. If that were true, Paul was confused and double-minded.

It was Paul who also reiterated many of the commandments that were written in the Old Testament. If he meant that all laws and ordinances were abolished then why did he talk of them in letters that he wrote to different churches? The answer is clear. The Ten Commandments were not abolished.

Paul in no way insinuated in any of his writings that any of the Ten Commandments had been invalidated. He actually said the complete opposite. He repeatedly verified the importance of the Ten Commandments. Once again, grace never annulled any of the Ten Commandments including the commandment of keeping the Sabbath Day holy.

Proper Interpretation for Proper Application

Any pastor who teaches on the Ten Commandments runs the risk that someone will become an extremist just like the Pharisees that lived in the days that Jesus walked the earth. Error always lives next door to truth. Any truth that is taken to an extreme will result in error. Likewise, any person who takes the commandment of keeping the Sabbath Day holy to an ex-treme position will fall into the ditch of legalism.

There are some basic principles that we must under-stand for there to be proper interpretation of this command-ment. The first is that God created the Sabbath for man to rest and be refreshed both spiritually and naturally. Secondly, that the Sabbath is not restricted to a certain day of the week. Thirdly, keeping the Sabbath Day holy is a spiritual issue of the heart that God wants to be acted out in the natural. The fourth principle is that doing work on the Sabbath Day is not totally forbidden. In my book **Planted**, I discuss these principles in great detail. We will not in this writing except for the principle that remembering the Sabbath is not restricted to a certain day of the week.

A Seventh Day—Not a Certain Day

The early church met together on the first day of the week. Most theologians acknowledge that Sunday became the day of observance for the Sabbath in the New Testament church. We must understand that the principle of remembering the Sabbath was not about a certain day of the week, but rather a seventh day during the week to rest and be refreshed. In other words, there needs to be a day that we personally take to rest.

In the culture we live in today, more businesses are closed on Sunday than any other day of the week. Many that are open on Sundays do not open until noon. It makes sense that Sunday would be the day that we observe as the seventh day to rest and be spiritually refreshed.

Many people fall into the ditch of legalism saying that the Sabbath must be observed on Saturday and thus miss the heart of the commandment. As was previously stated, the Sabbath is a seventh day. It is one day of a seven day week. It is intended to be a day of rest and refreshing. The important thing is that we take time to rest and be spiritually refreshed rather than a legalistic observance on a particular day.

Rest, Refreshing, and Reciprocation

We mentioned at the beginning of this chapter that the Sabbath had a three-fold purpose. First of all, it was to be a day of REST. Secondly, it was to be a day of REFRESHING. Thirdly, it was to be a day of RECIPROCATION.

Again, the Sabbath Day (a seventh day) was instituted at the time of creation. God is the first one who observed it. It was observed before the law was instituted. Then, during the giving of the Ten Commandments, God said, "REMEMBER the Sabbath day." Remember what He did.

Think about this. If God, who has all power, would take a rest, then certainly we should. God took a breather on the seventh day. God instituted this because He loved the man whom He had created.

It has been proven scientifically that those who do not get proper rest die prematurely. There are numerous medical issues that evolve from being a workaholic. That is not God's plan for any of our lives. Premature death is not what God desires for any of us. We all have a divine destiny that God desires for us to fulfill. God wants us to take a day to rest so that we can accomplish it.

Here is a very interesting fact. Research has proven that those who go to church regularly live on average eight years longer than those who do not. This could be due to many different factors that result from hearing the Word of God taught and worshiping the Lord. However, could it also be that someone is getting rest, both physical and spiritual, when they remember the Sabbath and go to church? Could it be that God knew what was best for us when He commanded us to take a day of rest?

Freshen Up

The second purpose for the Sabbath was REFRESHING. We need opportunity to be spiritually refreshed. When we come together as the body of Christ we are afforded the opportunity to minister one to another. There is spiritual refreshment that is released within our lives as we gather together for this purpose.

God's design is that we be invigorated by the Word and the ministry of the Holy Spirit. This takes place when we gather together as the Bible commands us. In Leviticus 23:3 we read the seventh day was to be a holy convocation. It was to be a time of meeting together for the purposes of worship, fellowship, and spiritual refreshing.

Sometimes, we may sense the need to "freshen up" after a day of work before we go somewhere for dinner at a restaurant. That means we may wash our face and hands, change our clothes, and spray on some cologne. Likewise, when we gather together as the church, we "freshen up" our spirit man. We receive the washing of the water of the Word. We put on the garment of praise for the spirit of heaviness. We start smelling different spiritually as we worship the Lord and get in His presence.

Understand that the writer of Hebrews rearticulates the fourth commandment in Hebrews chapter ten.

And let us consider one another in order to stir up love and good works, not forsaking the assembling of ourselves together, as is the manner of some, but exhorting one another, and so much the more as you see the Day approaching. For if we sin willfully after we

*have received the knowledge of the truth, there no
longer remains a sacrifice for sins (Hebrews 10:24-26).*

Here we see the purpose of the fourth commandment
being declared. The reason God said to "remember the Sabbath
day" was for the purpose of spiritual refreshing that was to be
received through meeting together. The writer of Hebrews emphasized the importance of assembling as the church. He goes
on to explain there were some in the church who had forsaken
the fourth commandment. They were not assembling together.

Considering One Another

Something interesting to note is that he said they should
"consider one another" by not forsaking assembling together.
We can actually see from this statement that failure to follow
the fourth commandment by not assembling together is a
selfish act. He said that to consider one another, or we could
say be considerate, you must gather together. If we stay home
in order to stay away from the gathering of the church we are
being selfish. Avoiding the assembling of the church makes a
statement that says, "I don't need anyone other than myself."

Another important thing to note is that immediately
after the exhortation to not forsake assembling together there is
an interesting statement made by the writer. He says, "For if we
sin willfully after we have received the knowledge of the
truth..." The writer of Hebrews gives an appeal to gather together and in essence obey the fourth commandment. Then he
says, "If we sin willfully." Could it be that when we refuse to
gather together and assemble (go to church) that we are
walking in disobedience? Could it be that it is willful sin?
Think about it.

God said at the beginning of creation "It is not good for
man to be alone." You were not created to function by yourself.
We all need others to accomplish the purpose of God for our

lives. There's an old saying that goes like this: it's the banana that gets separated from the bunch that gets peeled and eaten. Don't allow the devil to separate you from the church because his desire is to devour you. You need to stay planted and plugged into a local church body.

Day of Reciprocation

The third purpose for remembering the Sabbath Day was to be a day for RECIPROCATION. The Sabbath was designed to be a day of both giving and receiving. It was designed to be a time for the giving and receiving of tithes and offering. Also, there was to be opportunity for Christians to minister one to another as they gathered together. Giving and receiving was to be done in both spiritual things and natural things.

In Malachi chapter three, the prophet declares this:

"Bring all the tithes into the storehouse, That there may be food in My house, And try Me now in this," Says the LORD of hosts, "If I will not open for you the windows of heaven and pour out for you such blessing that there will not be room enough to receive it" (Malachi 3:10).

We can see the principle of reciprocation in this Scripture. He said to "bring the tithe...that there may be food." As we bring the tithe there is a spiritual reciprocation of spiritual food that is then released. We also see that the windows of heaven are opened and blessing is poured out! That sounds like prosperity to me! Get planted and prosper is what is being said.

The E-Factors

God designated one day a week to be a time when those who are in covenant with Him could be **encouraged, edified, and empowered**. These are the E-factors of church life.

We come to be encouraged and to encourage. The reality is that there is a tremendous amount of things that go on during a week that can discourage and drain. Therefore, we need a day that we can gather with those of like precious faith who can encourage us. Not only that, but you can be an encouragement to someone else.

The word "edify" means to build up and make strong. Every believer needs to be built up. Every believer needs to be made strong. Can you see why the enemy wants you to forget the Sabbath Day? He doesn't want you to be made strong; he wants you to be weak and ineffective.

Remembering the Sabbath will result in you becoming a strong believer. Remembering the Sabbath and going to church will cause you to be built up in the Lord. Herein we see the heart of the commandment.

We need to understand that a byproduct of remembering the Sabbath and going to church is that we will be empowered to do the will of God. When you go to church and assemble with other believers it causes God's power to be released within your life. The Bible declares that one puts a thousand to flight and two will put ten thousand to flight (Deuteronomy 32:30). That means that when Christians come together in the unity of the spirit there is a divine synergy that is ignited and released within our lives. It doesn't happen any other way.

My friend, God knew what He was doing when He commanded us to "remember the Sabbath Day to keep it holy." If we will obey His command, we will see His blessing released within our lives. The heart of this important command is for us to be planted in the house of the Lord so we can grow and flourish in every area of our lives. Get planted and prosper! There are great benefits in store for those who will obey.

Please pray this prayer with me:

Father God, I make a fresh commitment today to follow Your command to remember the Sabbath Day. I appropriate forgiveness for any place within my life where I have broken this command. I receive deliverance and healing as I renounce the hidden works of darkness.

Today, I make a fresh commitment to be planted in the house of the Lord. I choose to not forsake assembling with those of like precious faith. I choose to get connected in a local church body. Thank You for Your grace that empowers and enables me to fulfill your commandment. Thank You, Holy Spirit, for Your ability to live above sin. Sin will not have dominion over me. In the name of Jesus, I pray. Amen.

CHAPTER SEVEN
OBEDIENCE AND SUBMISSION

"Honor your father and your mother, that your days may be long upon the land which the LORD your God is giving you" (Exodus 20:12).

The fifth commandment has probably been quoted by parents more than any other. Parents will usually make sure that their children know this commandment. My wife and I have three children. When they were growing up in the house we spoke this to them and made sure they had put it to memory.

Interestingly enough, Paul refers to this commandment in the New Testament in his epistle to the Ephesians. Let's read what Paul said.

> *Children, obey your parents in the Lord, for this is right. "HONOR YOUR FATHER AND MOTHER," which is the first commandment with promise: "THAT IT MAY BE WELL WITH YOU AND YOU MAY LIVE LONG ON THE EARTH" (Ephesians 6:1-3).*

I think it's very interesting that Paul in his letter to the church at Ephesus quotes the fifth commandment. This begs me to ask the question, "Why would Paul quote this commandment?" The answer is clear and obvious. The fifth commandment is still applicable and in effect within the New Testament. Paul would not have used one of the Ten Commandments as an exhortation if it were not a part of the New Covenant.

The Heart of the Commandment

Again, as has been stated, every commandment has an underlying principle that governs it. We need to understand the heart of the Father within each commandment that He gave. As we hear God's heart on the matter, there is a positive motivation that will arise within our hearts. The underlying principle of this commandment is THE NECESSITY OF OBEDIENCE AND SUBMISSION.

When Paul quotes this commandment, he makes a point of emphasizing that this is the first commandment with promise. That promise is your life will go well and be extended here on earth. It is interesting to note that at the beginning of this book, the story was shared of the rich young ruler coming to Jesus and asking the question of what needed to be done to have eternal life. Jesus answered him by saying, "Keep the commandments."

The connection I want you to see is Paul talks about long LIFE in relationship to keeping the fifth commandment. Jesus talks about eternal LIFE in relationship to keeping all the commandments. The bottom line is this: obedience to the commandments result in LIFE! Death and destruction are the results of disobedience. "The wages of sin is death" (Romans 6:23).

We can readily see how the heart of the Father in this commandment is the principle of obedience. Paul begins this discourse in verse one by saying, "Children, OBEY." Then he quotes the commandment. In essence, before he states the command, he declares the heart of it. That is the necessity of obedience.

The Greek word used for "obey" in this passage of Scripture is *hupakouo̅* (hoop-ak-oo'-o). It means to hear under as a subordinate, to listen attentively; to heed or conform to a command or authority. When Paul says "obey" he is telling children to heed and conform to a command. "Do what you are told to do" is what he is telling them.

The First Authority

So why would God think it so important to institute as one of His top ten directives to all mankind to honor and obey their parents? It is because parental authority is the first authority that God ordained in the earth outside of His own. When God created man and woman, He told them to be fruitful and multiply; He commanded them to have a family. Within family there is order and authority. That authority within the home begins with the father and mother.

Before a child is ever introduced to civil authorities and its governing laws, they know the authority of their parents. Before a child learns about authority within the church, they will be acquainted with the authority of their parents. Before a child even learns about the authority of God and the Bible, they will experience the authority of their parents. The bottom line is parental authority is the first authority that we are introduced to as children.

The reason this is so important is the manner in which a child responds to the authority of their parents will determine how they respond to all authority. A child who disobeys their parents will disobey civil laws of society. A child who defies their parents will defy authorities within the church and their school. The fact is a child who dishonors their parents will also dishonor God. This is why God emphasizes within the Ten Commandments the importance of honoring and obeying our parents.

The Foundation of Society

The foundation of all society begins with the family. A family can only survive where there is order. The absence of order will bring chaos and mayhem. No family can survive in that environment. Therefore, no society, city, state or nation can survive without order in families and homes. That proper alignment begins with children obeying their parents.

There is no nation that can thrive in the midst of anarchy. If children are disobedient in the home, they will be disobedient in the community. If they are rebellious with their parents, they will rebel against law enforcement officials because they will rebel against law. Are you getting the picture? God frowns greatly on disobedience and blesses obedience. It is just that simple. We should do the same. Parents should do the same!

Today our prisons are full of people who were disobedient to their parents. The ones who primarily occupy the cells are those who dishonored their fathers and mothers. Most perpetrators of violent crimes are those who were disobedient to their parents. I'm not saying any of this to condemn anyone for past mistakes. I'm saying this so we will understand the importance of this commandment.

God did not speak this commandment just to hear His own voice. He said it so we would take heed, receive the blessing, and avoid the curse. Understand this; the heart of obedience and submission starts with children obeying their parents.

My wife and I raised three wonderful children. One thing that I would not allow within my children is rebellion. If I sensed rebellion, daddy would arise as a man of war just like God did in Exodus 15. I would immediately confront any spirit of rebellion that I saw or sensed. I understood that if I permitted that spirit to operate within my children, it would ultimately destroy them. If I were to give it an inch, it would take a mile.

Many parents today will not address these issues when they see them arise within their children. Some even think it's cute when their little three year old toddler sasses and speaks disrespectfully to others. When a parent fails to take action and address this kind of behavior they authorize it within the life of their child. There is nothing cute about rebellion and disrespect.

There are always challenges that parents face. Some face a higher degree of challenges than others. However, through the grace of God parents can overcome and triumph in every situation that they face.

The Way of the Transgressor Is Hard

"The law of the wise is a fountain of life, to depart from the snares of death. Good understanding giveth favour: but the way of transgressors is hard" (Proverbs 13:14-15, KJV).

Several things I want to point out in this passage of Scripture. The first is that transgressors (those who are disobedient) will have difficulty. When people decide to transgress law they are "cruising for a bruising." It's not God's plan that they suffer. However, God will not be mocked and whatever a man sows is what he will reap. The thinking that someone can live a lifestyle of disobedience and rebellion and still live in the blessing of God is a mockery of God!

Those who live in disobedience will suffer. The reality is that those who are in prison today are not there because they were law abiding citizens. They are there because they disobeyed the law. The people who get arrested and taken to jail are there because they have done something to violate a law. They are disobedient and much of it started when they were children at home.

Obedience is learned at an early age and so are rebellion and disobedience. It is the responsibility of parents to train up their children in the way of the Lord. The Bible declares, "Train up a child in the way that he should go and when he is old, he will not depart" (Proverbs 22:6). Parents must own that responsibility. It is fulfilled through precept, example, discipline, and love.

Godly Boundaries and Legitimate Control

Disobedience and rebellion are a problem in our nation today. We see it everywhere. We even see it in the church. If someone is given a directive and boundaries are established, the accusation begins to be hurled at leaders that they are being controlling. To a self-willed individual, any boundary established is controlling.

I finally got to the point where I said, "You are exactly right, I am going to control what goes on." Wow! What a shock that someone would say that. Parents have been given a responsibility to CONTROL their children. This is called being a parent. When I see young children who are wild and undisciplined, I'm upset with the parents rather than the kids.

There were times when some accused my wife and me of being overbearing and overprotective with our children. My response to them was, "These are my children to whom God gave me the responsibility." I was determined to be faithful to my first ministry which was my family. Today, all of our children are serving the Lord and actively involved in ministry. We took our responsibility seriously. If I could not be faithful with my kids, God would not let me pastor His. Think about it.

Pastors have a responsibility within the family of God to CONTROL what goes on within the local church by establishing biblical parameters and boundaries. That's called accepting the responsibility that has been delegated from the Lord. Anarchy should not be the rule. Everybody doing whatever they want to do was not the pattern of the early church. There should be godly Biblical control in that which takes place within a local church body.

What You Like Least and What You Need Most

That which you like the least is probably what you need the most. The people that seem to have a problem with teaching on giving are usually stingy people. The people that take exception to teaching on commitment to the church are the unfaithful ones. Likewise, the people who have the problem with authority and boundaries are usually the rebellious and obstinate.

Again, rebellious, disobedient, and self-willed people will always interpret boundaries, rules, or laws as being controlling. These same people, when confronted, will get upset and then suddenly hear the Lord speak to them that it's time for them to leave. It's amazing how that confrontation of improper behavior seems to prompt rebellious people to hear the words, "Time to leave."

Disobeying what one is instructed to do does not make a person strong. It doesn't make them their "own man." It actually makes them void of understanding. If you look back at the Scripture that we read previously, it contrasts someone with "good understanding" that produces favor versus the "way of the transgressor" which is hard. So when someone chooses to ignore instruction and be a transgressor they become someone who is void of understanding, and they bypass favor.

The only time that we see disobedience allowed is when someone is given a command that is in direct conflict with a pre-existing command from the Lord. Peter was commanded to stop preaching in the name of Jesus. He said "We ought to obey God rather than men" (Acts 5:29). Jesus had already told them to go into all the world and preach the gospel. He added that they were to cast out demons, heal the sick, and work miracles in His name—the name of Jesus. The governing body had told them to do something contradictory to that which Jesus had specifically told all the disciples. However, none of us can use that Scripture as a justification for disobeying a directive just because we don't like it or it brings a boundary within our life or ministry.

Obedience and Submission in the Workplace

Bondservants, be obedient to those who are your masters according to the flesh, with fear and trembling, in sincerity of heart, as to Christ; not with eyeservice, as men-pleasers, but as bondservants of Christ, doing the will of God from the heart, with goodwill doing service, as to the Lord, and not to men, knowing that whatever good anyone does, he will receive the same from the Lord, whether he is a slave or free (Ephesians 6:5-8).

Obedience and submission to authority is the plan and will of God. Simply put, do what you're told to do! Paul makes this very clear in his letter to the Ephesians.

Immediately after Paul articulates the commandment of honoring and obeying parents, he proceeds to give a directive of obedience concerning servants to their masters. A modern day application would be that of employees to their supervisors. So we observe Paul emphasizing the same principle contained in the fifth commandment as it relates in the workplace. Paul reveals the heart of the commandment which is the necessity of obedience and submission.

He goes on to say that there is a blessing associated with obedience. He declares that whatever good anyone does, he will receive the same back from the Lord. The seeds of obedience and submission that are sown will produce a great harvest within their lives. God will bless those who function with a submissive heart.

Unwilling to Obey

Samuel also said to Saul, "The LORD sent me to anoint you king over His people, over Israel. Now therefore, heed the voice of the words of the LORD. Thus says the LORD of hosts: 'I will punish Amalek for what he did to Israel, how he ambushed him on the way when he came up from Egypt. Now go and attack Amalek, and utterly destroy all that they have, and do not spare them. But kill both man and woman, infant and nursing child, ox and sheep, camel and donkey.'" And Saul attacked the Amalekites, from Havilah all the way to Shur, which is east of Egypt. He also took Agag king of the Amalekites alive, and utterly destroyed all the people with the edge of the sword. But Saul and the people spared Agag and the best of the sheep, the oxen, the fatlings, the lambs, and all that was good, and were unwilling to utterly destroy them. But everything despised and worthless, that they utterly destroyed" (1 Samuel 15:1-3, 7-9).

Here we see Saul given a specific command to totally destroy the Amalekites and everything within their land. Saul destroys all of the people with the exception of Agag. He also takes the best of the usable beasts and brings them back with him. There is a key word that is used in verse nine that I want to bring to your attention. That is the word **unwilling**. Saul was unwilling to do what God had commanded. He was unwilling to obey fully.

When someone is unwilling, their own will is being exalted. Saul had exalted his will above the will of God. He had exalted his own desire above the desire of the Lord. Anytime that anyone exalts their own fleshly will above the will of God it is sin. It actually is the sin of rebellion.

If we think our ideas are better than God's, it culminates in the sin of rebellion. Saul thought he had a better idea. He felt his human reasoning was greater than the Word of the Lord. He believed his political posturing was more important than the authority that God had already given him.

Let's continue to read this passage to see the end result:

> Then Samuel went to Saul, and Saul said to him, "Blessed are you of the LORD! I have performed the commandment of the LORD." But Samuel said, "What then is this bleating of the sheep in my ears, and the lowing of the oxen which I hear?" And Saul said, "They have brought them from the Amalekites; for the people spared the best of the sheep and the oxen, to sacrifice to the LORD your God; and the rest we have utterly destroyed." Then Samuel said to Saul, "Be quiet! And I will tell you what the LORD said to me last night." And he said to him, "Speak on." So Samuel said, "When you were little in your own eyes, were you not head of the tribes of Israel? And did not the LORD anoint you king over Israel? Now the LORD sent you on a mission, and said, 'Go, and utterly destroy the sinners, the Amalekites, and fight against them until they are consumed.' Why then did you not obey the voice of the LORD? Why did you swoop down on the spoil, and do evil in the sight of the LORD?"

And Saul said to Samuel, "But I have obeyed the voice of the LORD, and gone on the mission on which the LORD sent me, and brought back Agag king of Amalek; I have utterly destroyed the Amalekites. But the people took of the plunder, sheep and oxen, the best of the things which should have been utterly destroyed, to sacrifice to the LORD your God in Gilgal." So Samuel said: "Has the LORD as great delight in burnt offerings and sacrifices, As in obeying the voice of the LORD? Behold, to obey is better than sacrifice, And to heed than the fat of rams. For rebellion is as the sin of witchcraft, And stubbornness is as iniquity and idolatry. Because you have rejected the word of the LORD, He also has rejected you from being king." Then Saul said to Samuel, "I have sinned, for I have transgressed the commandment of the LORD and your words, because I feared the people and obeyed their voice. Now therefore, please pardon my sin, and return with me, that I may worship the LORD." But Samuel said to Saul, "I will not return with you, for you have rejected the word of the LORD, and the LORD has rejected you from being king over Israel." And as Samuel turned around to go away, Saul seized the edge of his robe, and it tore. So Samuel said to him, "The LORD has torn the kingdom of Israel from you today, and has given it to a neighbor of yours, who is better than you" (1 Samuel 15:13-28).

The Sin of Rebellion

There are so many truths that can be derived from this story. But this is the primary one that I want you to see. Rebellion is always sin. It will produce disastrous results. The prophet Samuel told King Saul that rebellion is as the sin of witchcraft. As a result of King Saul's rebellion, he lost his throne. He was tormented by demonic spirits because of his partial obedience. Understand that rebellion will cause one to be tormented. It will not produce the peace and blessing of God.

When King Saul rebelled against God, Samuel said, "To obey is better than sacrifice and to heed than the fat of rams." One translation says, "God doesn't want your sacrifice. He wants you to obey Him" (CEV). God wants obedience more than anything else.

The Test of Obedience and Submission

Obeying something that you want to do is easy. If someone were to give me a command to eat a piece of cheesecake, I would have no problem at all obeying it. However, if someone gave me a command to eat caviar, I would have great difficulty obeying that directive. The fact is I like cheesecake, and I don't like caviar. So, eating cheesecake presents no challenge to submission. However, eating caviar would present a challenge to me.

I'm using this example to illustrate this point. Obedience and submission are tested only when one is given a command or directive that they do not want to do. Anyone can obey when the directive is something pleasant. The question becomes what is one going to do when it is unpleasant? How will you respond when the command goes against your personal taste and preference? We must learn to obey even when our flesh is saying "No!"

The fact is this: if one only obeys when it feels good then they will ultimately rebel. Situational obedience produces partial obedience. This is what happened to King Saul. He obeyed partially. However, Samuel called it rebellion. God calls situational and partial obedience rebellion. Think about it.

Submission will be tested in the place that you disagree. It's easy to submit to that which you agree. It's difficult when you don't agree. It's easy to go the speed limit when you think it's reasonable. However, people have difficulty if they think it's unreasonable. Again, situational obedience is rebellion. It is deceptive because those who operate in this manner feel they are justified.

The Fleshly Justification of Rebellion

Saul felt as if he was justified in his rebellion. After all, it was for a good cause. They were going to use the sheep and oxen for making sacrifices unto the Lord. Besides that, the people wanted Saul to do this. However, his natural justifications for his partial obedience did not measure up to the command that had been given. Therefore, it was rebellion. Fleshly justifications will never measure up and at the end of the day the Lord will say the same thing: "This is rebellion."

My personal opinion is that fleshly justification and excuses are the most dangerous things that any believer can embrace. Saul, when confronted by Samuel, continued to try to justify himself. He made excuses for himself and even blamed others for his disobedience.

In contrast, King David sinned to what I would consider a greater degree. He committed adultery with Bathsheba and had her husband killed after he found out she was pregnant with his child. This was worse than Saul, in my opinion. However, when David was confronted by the prophet Nathan he said, "I am the man."

What a remarkable difference between the response of Saul and David. Saul blamed everyone else and David took responsibility for his actions. David could have said, "Well, she shouldn't have been on her rooftop taking a bath in plain sight." He could have said, "Well, it takes two to tango, and she's just as much at fault as me," but he didn't.

God forgave David because he accepted responsibility for his sin. God ripped the kingdom from Saul because he lied and blamed everyone else for his own failure. Saul's self-justification was rooted in rebellion. His rebellion ended up being his downfall.

Saul had missed out on the heart of the fifth commandment. He should have obeyed the word of the Lord given by the prophet. It was not just a man giving him a directive; it was a man delivering a command to him that had been sent from God. When he disobeyed the voice of the prophet he rebelled against God.

It is important that we catch the heart of this important commandment. It is important that we obey those in authority. It is imperative that we live with a submissive spirit. We will see God's blessing manifested within our lives as we adhere to the commandment of honoring our father and mother.

Please pray this prayer with me:

Father God, I make a fresh commitment today to obey Your command to honor my parents and obey authorities. I appropriate forgiveness for any place within my life where I have broken this command. I receive deliverance and healing as I renounce the hidden works of darkness.

Today, I forsake any and all types of rebellion, disobedience, and self-will. I choose to be obedient and submissive. I forsake living life in a rebellious manner, and I humble myself under Your mighty hand today. Thank You for Your grace that empowers and enables me to fulfill Your commandment. Thank You, Holy Spirit, for Your ability to live above sin. Sin will not have dominion over me. In the name of Jesus, I pray. Amen.

CHAPTER EIGHT
FORGIVE AND DITCH THE ANGER

"You shall not murder."
(Exodus 20:13)

The sixth commandment is the first commandment of the second tablet. It also represents the first moral law broken in human existence. It is very simple: do not murder another human being. This is not only a part of moral law that was dictated in the Ten Commandments, but is a civil law in every civilized society known to man. I do not know of anyone who would say that this is not an applicable commandment for us in the New Testament. The law concerning murder has not changed from the Old Testament to the New. It is reemphasized in the New Testament.

Let's see what Jesus says about this commandment:

"Do not think that I came to destroy the Law or the Prophets. I did not come to destroy but to fulfill. For assuredly, I say to you, till heaven and earth pass away,

one jot or one tittle will by no means pass from the law till all is fulfilled. Whoever therefore breaks one of the least of these commandments, and teaches men so, shall be called least in the kingdom of heaven; but whoever does and teaches them, he shall be called great in the kingdom of heaven. For I say to you, that unless your righteousness exceeds the righteousness of the scribes and Pharisees, you will by no means enter the kingdom of heaven. You have heard that it was said to those of old, 'YOU SHALL NOT MURDER, and whoever murders will be in danger of the judgment.' But I say to you that whoever is angry with his brother without a cause shall be in danger of the judgment. And whoever says to his brother, 'Raca!' shall be in danger of the council. But whoever says, 'You fool!' shall be in danger of hell fire. Therefore if you bring your gift to the altar, and there remember that your brother has something against you, leave your gift there before the altar, and go your way. First be reconciled to your brother, and then come and offer your gift. Agree with your adversary quickly, while you are on the way with him, lest your adversary deliver you to the judge, the judge hand you over to the officer, and you be thrown into prison. Assuredly, I say to you, you will by no means get out of there till you have paid the last penny" (Matthew 5:17-26).

I would like to take this opportunity to discuss several things that Jesus brings to light in this passage of Scripture. A tremendous amount of revelation is contained in these ten verses. I believe that every word that Jesus spoke was designed to bring spiritual understanding and reveal the heart of the Father God.

Jesus Goes to the Heart of the Matter

Jesus continually said that He did not come to do His own will, but rather the will of the Father. He said that the miracles and healings that He performed were done by the Father. He said that He came in order that the Father would be glorified. Jesus always pointed back to the Father. He was submitted and obedient to the Father God.

The first thing that I want to point out is the overarching principle that we see taking place. Jesus takes this commandment to the next level. He raises the standard and explains the heart of the Father within the commandment. Jesus points out that the commandment is more than refraining from killing someone.

In verse twenty Jesus says something very interesting. He says, "Unless your righteousness exceeds the righteousness of the scribes and Pharisees, you will by no means enter into the kingdom of God." What's interesting about this statement is that the Pharisees prided themselves on being keepers of the law. They obeyed the letter of the law. However, they had missed the heart of the Father within the commandments.

Jesus goes on to explain how that they had heard the letter of the law of the commandment—the exact words that were stated. However, He says the commandment is more than just what is stated on the surface. He tells them that He is raising the bar. The standard is more than merely abstaining from the act of physically murdering someone.

Jesus declares the heart of the Father within this commandment and the spiritual principle that governs it. He says that you cannot be angry with your brother without cause. He even goes on to say that the punishment is equal—that being, judgment would ensue.

Jesus Addresses the Root

Jesus begins to deal with the results of anger that are just as bad as murder. Words that come out of our mouth that tear down another person can be as bad as physical murder. Our words should be edifying one another rather than destroying one another. Our words should be sweet like honey rather than sour like lemons.

This is what happens many times when people allow anger to rule their lives. Jesus said that out of the abundance of the heart the mouth would speak. When anyone allows anger and offense to have root within their heart, it results in harmful words coming out of their mouths. These words can cut others to the core of their being and do great damage to their own self-worth. Jesus said that this is sinful and will have negative ramifications in the lives of those who do it.

Jesus addresses that which is at the root of anger and murder which is offense and unforgiveness. He begins to deal with the process of handling offense. Let's look again at what Jesus said concerning this.

"Therefore if you bring your gift to the altar, and there remember that your brother has something against you, leave your gift there before the altar, and go your way. First be reconciled to your brother, and then come and offer your gift" (Matthew 5:23-24).

Relationship Is More Important

Jesus said that if you know your brother is angry with you or offended, it is more important that you be reconciled than give your gift. Jesus placed the emphasis on relationship rather than our gift. He stated the paramount objective to be reconciliation and peace with our brother.

Let me share this a little differently. Jesus says that your relationship with your brothers and sisters in Christ is more important than your ministry gift functioning within the church. Our ministry becomes vain when we have unresolved issues with others in the church. If you know there is dissension between you and someone else in the church then go be reconciled. Get it right! Kiss and make up! Stop hanging on to the offense and forgive if you are angry about something.

In verse twenty-four Jesus says to be RECONCILED. In verse twenty-five he says to AGREE.

"Agree with your adversary quickly, while you are on the way with him, lest your adversary deliver you to the judge, the judge hand you over to the officer, and you be thrown into prison. Assuredly, I say to you, you will by no means get out of there till you have paid the last penny" (Matthew 5:25-26).

Right or Reconciled

Find a place of agreement so there can be reconciliation. Remember it is more important to be reconciled than be right. In valuable relationships, you are better to be reconciled than be right and divided.

Many times within husband and wife relationships things can spin out of control. Words can begin to be hurled at each other when anger and offense take dominion in the household. Most of the time, these explosions take place over trivial matters. These are needless arguments that result in nothing but hurt feelings and tumultuous emotional roller-coaster rides.

It seems as though in these situations no one is willing to come into agreement with the other because it's too important to both of them to be right. Is it really that important to be declared that you were right? Wouldn't you rather have peace and joy in the home than get a pretend medal for being right? Think about it.

Jesus said to agree with your adversary quickly. Once again Jesus gave us a spiritual principle to govern our lives. Don't live your life as a brawler. Choose to be a person who agrees rather than looking for an argument. Why argue and fight when you can live peacefully?

Jesus further stated that living as an uncooperative and disagreeable person will have consequences. He said that you ultimately go to prison. Those of us who are married know exactly what the Lord was talking about. We call it the "dog house." Jesus said the price of this kind of behavior is very costly. In other words, IT'S NOT WORTH IT! Agree and be reconciled.

The reality is if we walk around angry we only hurt ourselves. Walking in anger and offense is like taking poison while expecting someone else to die. It doesn't work that way. If you take the poison, you will die. Walking around angry is hazardous to your spiritual health.

Hatred and Envy

For this is the message that you heard from the beginning, that we should love one another, not as Cain who was of the wicked one and murdered his brother. And why did he murder him? Because his works were evil and his brother's righteous. We know that we have passed from death to life, because we love the brethren. He who does not love his brother abides in death. Whoever hates his brother is a murderer, and you know that no murderer has eternal life abiding in him (1 John 3:11-12, 14-15).

John points out in this passage of Scripture that the root of murder is hatred. Murder begins with hatred. He is basically saying, 'Don't be a hater.' Hating is sin. Not only is it sin, but it is dangerous and produces bad fruit within those in whom it operates.

John asks the question why did Cain murder Abel? Then he answers the question, "Because his works were evil and his brother's righteous." John gives us insight as to why Cain committed murder. He was envious of his brother's acceptance from the Lord. This was offensive to Cain and ultimately produced bitterness and hatred which led him to commit murder.

The Root of Offense and Jealousy

Hatred is not necessarily the result of someone doing something evil that could be considered deserving of being hated. John says that Abel's works were righteous. He had done nothing wrong. He had offered an acceptable sacrifice to the Lord. Cain is upset about Abel's sacrifice being accepted. Anger and hatred are the result of a taken offense.

To get greater insight, let's examine the original account of this in Genesis.

> And in the process of time it came to pass that Cain brought an offering of the fruit of the ground to the LORD. Abel also brought of the firstborn of his flock and of their fat. And the LORD respected Abel and his offering, but He did not respect Cain and his offering. And Cain was very angry, and his countenance fell. So the LORD said to Cain, "Why are you angry? And why has your countenance fallen? If you do well, will you not be accepted? And if you do not do well, sin lies at the door. And its desire is for you, but you should rule over it" (Genesis 4:3-7).

Notice what is said in verse five. "Cain was very angry and his countenance fell." Here again we see the root of murder. Cain got angry about the situation. His anger was rooted in offense that stemmed from jealousy. Abel had done nothing to Cain. Abel had not assaulted Cain physically or verbally. Abel is obeying God. His works are righteous and God accepts his sacrifice.

The Hebrew word translated "angry" in this Scripture is defined to blaze up of anger, zeal, or jealousy. Again, we see there is an issue with jealousy within Cain that causes an offense that pushes him to commit murder. The Bible says that jealousy is as cruel as the grave (Song of Solomon 8:6). Why is that? It's because jealousy and envy produce anger and hatred that bring forth the fleshly work of murder.

God tells Cain, "Sin lies at the door and its desire is for you, but you should rule over it." The Hebrew word translated "sin" is defined as an offense. With that in mind, let's read this Scripture. "An OFFENSE lies at the door and its desire is for you, but you should rule over it."

I believe God was warning Cain of something transpiring in his life. He told Cain that if he would do well his sacrifice would be accepted. Obviously, Cain had not offered an acceptable sacrifice. I believe that God was saying, "Cain, you need to get a grip and take control of your mind and emotions and then offer up an acceptable sacrifice."

God was giving Cain a second chance. He was giving him another opportunity to make things right. He also warned Cain that he needed to get rid of his offense and not let it rule him. However, Cain didn't. Cain hung on to his anger and offense and did the exact opposite of what God told him.

Get Over It!

Cain needed to "get over it." Cain had an opportunity to offer a sacrifice that would be acceptable. His problem was he couldn't "get over it." Cain could have bypassed murdering his brother. However, he couldn't "get over it."

I know that the words "get over it" have the potential of sounding cold, unfeeling, and uncompassionate. However, regardless of our situation, we must learn to "get over it." The key is love and forgiveness. Is there anyone who has never had someone else wrong them? Is there anyone who has never experienced something undesirable that they had to "get over?" The answer to both of those questions is "No!" We have all experienced unpleasant things perpetrated by others whom we love and possess close relationship. However, for those relationships to continue we had to "get over it."

Forgiveness vs. Holding On

The reality is that Jesus commanded us to "get over it." He said that we should be reconciled and come into agreement. If you hold on to offense this cannot be done. You have to "get over it." The primary key is walking in forgiveness.

Holding on to a past offense will only cause one to experience that pain repeatedly. It will be something that haunts continually. It will cause misery and torment as bitterness, anger, and hatred take hold of one's life. My friend, it's not worth it.

Many hold on to an offense and stay angry because they think they are exacting revenge on the perpetrator. However, they only hurt themselves. Being angry and bitter at others will only cause you to suffer. Why put yourself through this when you can forgive and be healed?

Understand that forgiveness is a command and not an option. Jesus commanded us to forgive. He went on to say that if we would not forgive, the Father would not forgive us (Mark 11:25). The bottom line is if we don't forgive others we reject our own forgiveness. Are you willing to reject your own forgiveness at the price of holding on to an offense?

Forgiveness by Faith

Forgiving requires faith because you forgive by faith. Forgiveness starts with the words of your mouth. To forgive you must express it with that which you say. Begin to speak it out. Forgiveness must be articulated before it will be demonstrated.

The Bible says that "death and life are in the power of the tongue" (Proverbs 18:21). You must declare it even when you don't feel it.

Forgiveness is not based upon feeling or emotion. When you first forgive someone you may not feel any forgiveness. Many times it takes some time for our feelings to catch up with the initial act of forgiveness. However, if we will be faithful to express it, the feelings of forgiveness will eventually manifest.

I have seen those who were holding on to anger and offenses receive their healing and deliverance the moment they forgave. Forgiveness opened the door for God to manifest His power within their lives. It cleared the way for God to release His blessing within their lives.

Dangers of Failure to Forgive

"If you forgive the sins of any, they are forgiven them; if you retain the sins of any, they are retained" (Job 20:23).

In this verse of Scripture, Jesus shares the most dangerous result of not forgiving someone. He says that failure to forgive (retaining someone's sin), causes those sins to be retained. This means if we fail to forgive someone then that sin becomes ours. We will act out the same sin if we fail to forgive. So the act that you despised being committed to you will be that which you ultimately commit.

Jesus was serious about forgiveness. He repeatedly made clear the necessity of forgiving. The reason for this is that failure to forgive actually hurts the hurting. The worst thing for a person hurting is more hurt. Failure to forgive becomes the thing that keeps hurting. It becomes the continual movie that plays within one's mind that revives every negative emotion and feeling that was experienced at the time of the event. Failure to forgive is like salt in a wound.

I've told our congregation that unpleasant things happen while living on earth. That's not a negative statement or confession. That is just the reality of living in a fallen world. It's like the old shows on television that depicted a baby being born. The doctor would hold it upside down and then swat it on the bottom. Welcome to earth!

The reality is unpleasant things do happen. Jesus said that in the world you would have tribulation (John 16:33). The good news is He didn't stop there. He said, "Be of good cheer for I have overcome the world." You can overcome through the faith and love of God. You don't have to hang on to the hurt and anger of the past. You can release it through forgiveness.

My friend, GET OVER IT! Forgive and start moving forward. There is no future in anger and hatred. Jesus said that it would eventually send you to prison, spiritually and possibly naturally. God has greater plans for your life than to live being tormented for the rest of your days on the earth. He has a destiny and purpose that you are to fulfill.

Ask yourself these questions. Do I want my future controlled by someone who may have hurt me? Is it worth it? I trust that your answer to both of these questions is "No." Now, make the choice to forgive and receive His healing.

Please pray this prayer with me:

Father God, I make a fresh commitment today to follow Your command to not be filled with anger and hatred which is murder. I appropriate forgiveness for any place within my life where I have broken this command. I receive deliverance and healing as I renounce the hidden works of darkness.

Today, I forsake any and all types of hatred and anger that may be rooted in unforgiveness, offense, envy or anything else that is fleshly and ungodly. I choose to forgive and release any unrighteous anger in my life. I choose to walk in love towards any who may have wronged me. Thank You for Your grace that empowers and enables me to fulfill Your commandment. Thank You for power and ability to live above sin. Sin will not have dominion over me. In Jesus name. Amen.

CHAPTER NINE
COVENANT KEEPERS

"You shall not commit adultery."
(Exodus 20:14)

The seventh commandment of the Ten Commandments deals with sexual sin. Technically, adultery is sex outside of marriage involving one who is married. However, I do believe this commandment involves any type of sexual involvement outside of the Biblically defined marriage relationship of one man and one woman. Therefore, any type of sexual relationship other than that between a man and woman who are married to each other is sin.

It seems as though our society today has become an "anything goes" culture. There appears to be no absolutes, and everything is just "shades of gray." People have lost their way. Many Christians have lost their way too! I believe the reason for this is that the only person who has the ability to establish a moral compass within our lives has been left out of the equation as it pertains to sex.

God Had Something to Say About Sex

The reality is that God had a lot to say about sex. It is all throughout the word of God. God was very specific about this area of human existence; He began His instruction at the time of creation. God was not silent about this. He never expected us to figure it out all by ourselves and make our own rules as we went along. God dictated with who, what, and when sex was right and wrong. We will discuss these things in more detail later within this chapter.

We must understand that God never said, "Do what you want to do, and if it feels good, go for it." It's amazing to hear some of the people in the world today who propagate the line of thinking which says, "As long as it's consenting adults, then it's all right." Nothing could be further from the truth.

So let's see what Jesus has to say about the seventh commandment.

"You have heard that it was said to those of old, 'YOU SHALL NOT COMMIT ADULTERY.' But I say to you that whoever looks at a woman to lust for her has already committed adultery with her in his heart. If your right eye causes you to sin, pluck it out and cast it from you; for it is more profitable for you that one of your members perish, than for your whole body to be cast into hell. And if your right hand causes you to sin, cut it off and cast it from you; for it is more profitable for you that one of your members perish, than for your whole body to be cast into hell. Furthermore it has been said, 'Whoever divorces his wife, let him give her a certificate of divorce.' But I say to you that whoever divorces his wife for any reason except sexual immorality causes her to commit adultery; and whoever marries a woman who is divorced commits adultery" (Matthew 5:27-32).

The Heart of the Commandment

In this passage of Scripture Jesus expounds on the seventh commandment. In doing so, He brings understanding to the heart of the commandment. Jesus also reveals how that the commandment is more than refraining from the physical act only. Jesus raises the standard.

The fact that Jesus begins to talk about divorce in relationship to adultery reveals that He is expounding on the heart of the commandment. The heart of the commandment involves the issues of covenant and commitment. The fact is that adultery and divorce are the end result of covenant breaking. Adultery and divorce are the result of commitments being annulled.

The world we live in today is full of shallow commitments. The commitment level of most people today extends to the point where they feel they are benefited. However, once they feel as though they are no longer being benefited, they leave. They forget the covenant and promise they made; they are "fair weather friends." It is very unfortunate.

Jesus Addresses the Origin of Adultery

When Jesus spoke about adultery He stated that everyone was already familiar with the letter of the law. He said, "You have heard...do not commit adultery." Jesus realized He was teaching people who were already familiar with the law. However, He realized they had missed the heart of the Father in the commandment. So, He brings expansion and clarity to the commandment.

Jesus says that adultery does not start with the physical act of sex with an individual to whom one is not married. He says it starts with the eye and the heart. Jesus makes it clear that when someone allows sexual lust to be stirred through looking at someone else with sexual desire that they commit adultery in their heart. He was stating that adultery is not merely a physical act; it is a matter of the heart.

The reality is that when someone who is married looks on an individual to whom they are not married and desires them sexually there is a breaking of covenant. It is betrayal; it is sin. It is devaluing to the party who is betrayed and opens the door for great mistrust.

One day, I was watching a Christian television program. A husband and wife who pastored a church were hosting the show and they were talking about marriage. As they began to talk to another guest on the show, much to my surprise, the wife said that she did not have a problem with her husband admiring beautiful women. She said that she would think something was wrong with him if he didn't. Several years later they divorced.

Do you wonder what happened? Jesus already answered that question. He expressed the danger of "admiring" the beautiful people in the world. I say that with a degree of sarcasm because of the ignorance and deception of the wife who said she had no problem with her husband "admiring" other women. She should have had a problem with it! Jesus had a problem with it! Why shouldn't she?

For some unknown reason there are those in the church today who believe they know more than Jesus. Although they would never admit to this, their actions and words are evidence that they do. Many people quote the Word when it is expedient for them, yet they ignore and invalidate it when it's not. My friend, none of us can ever change the words of Jesus and expect to come out good on the other side of that kind of behavior.

There is a reason that Jesus said, 'Don't look.' He made it plain that adultery would be the end result. The truth is when adultery is committed in the heart because of continual looking and sexual meditation, it is only a few more steps before it will be acted out in the bedroom.

My wife and I have counseled many married couples in our ministry. Fortunately, we have had very few cases of adultery that we have had to address. The one thing I can tell you from the cases we have dealt with is that none of them happened as the result of a single momentary encounter. It is not as if someone is walking down the street and then five minutes later they are in bed with someone to whom they are not married.

Sexual Meditation

Adultery happens as the result of sexual meditation. Sometimes it may start with flirting in the workplace. Then it becomes a lunch date with a business partner. From there it becomes consistent conversing over non-business issues that involves how their spouse just doesn't understand them. The next thing you know they are hugging each other in an attempt to console one another while they cope with their miserable situations and circumstances. Then the sexual proposal is initiated since neither one of them are really being satisfied by their spouse. Within their minds, this brings justification to the illicitness of their affair.

This is just one example of how adultery happens. The whole process does not usually happen in a five minute window. If it does, then the spirit of adultery and sexual perversion has hold of someone to the point of demonic possession. However, the norm is that sexual sin starts in the mind and heart long before it is acted out in the bed.

This is one of the reasons that pornography is such a danger. Pornography is sinful sexual meditation. It is where someone gives their mind and heart over to looking at something that God has forbidden them to have because it produces covenant breaking.

The Deceptiveness of Sin

We must understand that sin is deceptive. Sin does not announce, "Sin is here!" Sin hides itself. Sin makes itself appealing. Sin will attempt to justify itself. Sin will make excuses. Sin will promise satisfaction.

Sin will not tell you, "I am here to destroy you." Sin does not announce that it will cause division in your home and family. Sin doesn't tell you that your job will now be in jeopardy. Sin doesn't tell you that the satisfaction lasts briefly to only be followed by condemnation.

If people could really see and discern the result of sin they would run from it. However, the lure of that which has been forbidden traps many people. It traps the unsaved and the saved. It doesn't have to be that way. We need to realize that the grace of God is present to empower and enable us to both discern sin and live above it. Hallelujah!

Grace Raises the Bar

Again, Jesus reemphasizes the seventh commandment. He also takes it to the next level. Grace raises the bar because it enables us to accomplish what the letter of the law never empowered anyone to do. The law revealed sin, but grace and the power of the Holy Spirit give us the ability to fulfill the "righteous requirement of the law."

Jesus connected lust, adultery, and divorce together. He revealed that these are the result of the breaking of covenant and commitment. This is the heart of the commandment. Keep the covenants and commitments that you make. Understand that the marriage covenant is the most important commitment you ever make, withstanding your commitment to the Lord.

The Pain of Divorce and Adultery

Marriages today are failing at an alarming rate. Approximately fifty percent of all marriages end in divorce. That is a pathetic statistic. Most marriages end because of what is called "irreconcilable differences." This basically means too much pride, unforgiveness, or sin in the relationship.

Many of these marriages end because of adultery. When one is unfaithful to their partner it is possibly the greatest betrayal that can be perpetrated. It is extremely painful and difficult for the other spouse to work through. Jesus Himself gave justification for divorce in cases where adultery is present. However, God can heal and restore in every situation.

We have seen God restore marriages and homes where adultery has taken place. In every situation, the individual who was victimized had to rely wholly on the grace of God. The emotional challenges that they encountered were many. However, God was faithful and brought healing to them and restoration to their marriages.

I recognize that not every marriage that has encountered adultery comes out on the other side with a testimony of victory. So, there is absolutely no condemnation to anyone who has suffered divorce because of an unfaithful partner. They are not under any kind of guilt or responsibility in these situations. But I do believe God will heal and restore homes even when there has been adultery.

God's Best Standard

God's best is that a man and woman get married and there be no adultery. This is the standard that God established. It's not too difficult either. The bottom line is this; when you are around anyone that is not your spouse, KEEP YOUR PANTS ON! Keep your eyes where they're supposed to be.

People contemplate and think about adultery long before they do it. It becomes an obsession with them to the point that they cannot clearly see spiritually. Understand that lust will hinder correct judgment. Lust will blind you. That's the reason Jesus said to keep your eyes straight ahead. Wandering eyes will destroy you.

Going back to the words of Jesus: He said that the command is not merely refrain from having sex with someone to whom you are not married; He says that you are to evade looking in that direction. Don't go there. It is the nullification of a commitment that one made. Ultimately, it will cause division and divorce. It will cause a covenant to be broken. So the heart of the commandment is about staying in covenant, keeping commitments, and remaining faithful.

Understanding Covenant

The divorce rate in America alone reveals that we have little understanding of covenant. Most teaching concerning covenant has to do with that which God has made available to us through the sacrifice of Jesus. Hardly anything is taught on covenant in relationship regarding our responsibility to the Lord.

Covenant is not a one-way street. God has given everything to us. Our side of the deal is we give everything to Him. He withholds nothing; we agree to withhold nothing. He loved us. We respond by loving Him. I trust you understand what I'm getting at. Covenant is bidirectional. There is an exchange in a covenant relationship.

Every successful relationship is based upon the principle of mutual benefiting. Anytime one party begins to feel slighted it places a strain on the relationship. If it is not addressed, the relationship will end up broken. Nothing in life is ever intended to be one person doing all of the giving and the other doing all of the taking. That is not covenant.

My wife and I have been married now for 32 years. When we were married, I made a covenant with her. At the same time, she made covenant with me. We declared promises to one another. We committed to one another. I promised to love and cherish her as Christ loves the church. She promised to be a faithful wife. There was a dialogue rather than a monologue.

Many people approach relationships from the aspect of what they can get out of it. They want to minimize their commitment and maximize the commitment of others to them. This is the indication of failure to understand covenant. In covenant there is equal commitment. There is equal contribution. There is a sharing of responsibilities and privileges.

Since there has been little understanding of covenant within the church, we see selfishness manifesting within the lives of many. Not only is there selfishness, but there are lukewarm hearts throughout.

One of the characteristics of the lukewarm church is that they live in denial of the truth while being deceived about their own spiritual condition. They say they are on fire (faithful) while they are actually ice cold (unfaithful). They say they are really committed to their marriage while they still engage in looking where they should not. They say they love their spouse while they fantasize about others.

Ultimately these people are spewed out of the mouth of God. They "taste" bad. You only spit out that which tastes bad. They taste bad to God, and they taste bad to those who are around them. There is nothing that tastes good about unfaithfulness and adultery. Although it is glamorized in Hollywood movies, it tastes bad if you partake of it.

The Need for Commitment

Jesus emphasizes the need for covenant and commitment. He reveals that adultery and divorce are rooted in the breaking of covenant and commitment. You may ask, "Which of these precedes the other, covenant breaking or adultery?" They are, in actuality, the same thing. Adultery is breaking covenant. Illicit sexual desire and meditation is transgression of a commitment.

Many today feel that as long as they "don't touch" there is acceptability in their actions. They believe that their deviance is minimized providing they refrain from having sexual intercourse. Jesus said something different. Jesus said it's the same transgression. He said that it was equally sin. He said that looking is equal to touching.

Just to emphasize that which we have been saying from the beginning of this book, all of the Ten Commandments are restated in the New Testament. Adultery was sin in the Old Testament and is still sin in the New Testament. The Apostle Paul went so far as to say that those who practice it would not inherit the kingdom of God. Although the kingdom of God has been defined differently by various ones, I do not believe that being disinherited from the kingdom of God is a good thing. So we are best to flee from the sin of adultery in all of its forms.

Sexual Perversion in the Culture

Unfortunately, one can hardly turn on the television today without seeing some type of sexual perversion being demonstrated or flaunted. Whether it is network television or cable/satellite services, the programming of today's television is filled with adultery, fornication, homosexuality, and all other abominations. However, many Christians have become so calloused and jaded that it no longer affects them in a way that would cause them to change the channel, boycott the station, or be righteously enraged that these kinds of things are being broadcast.

We witness programming and movies where profanity and all sorts of evil are portrayed and it no longer causes believers to even flinch. There is something wrong with this picture. The problem is that sin is deceptive. It promises that "you are only watching a movie" while the seed of that sin is being sown into your heart. We go to church on Sunday for one to two hours and hear the Word of God taught and then watch twenty or more hours of programming filled with bad news, profanity, sexual perversion, and lies. No wonder there is the proliferation of sin in the church today.

I am not attempting to only tell you the problem because I believe there is a solution. However, we must identify what is happening if we are going to bring applicable biblical solutions. The prophets we read about throughout the Bible would identify the sin and problems. They would also bring a word of redemption that would require repentance and change. It is time for the church to repent and change.

The solution to the problem we have today is evident. Get back to the Word of God and avoid things that are violations of the Ten Commandments. Those commandments give us a pathway of righteousness and a moral compass. God's commandments that are now written upon the tablets of our heart should light the way for us if we will allow.

Jesus Defines the Composition of the Marriage Covenant

The Pharisees also came to Him, testing Him, and saying to Him, "Is it lawful for a man to divorce his wife for just any reason?" And He answered and said to them, "Have you not read that He who made them at the beginning 'MADE THEM MALE AND FEMALE,' and said, 'FOR THIS REASON A MAN SHALL LEAVE

HIS FATHER AND MOTHER AND BE JOINED TO HIS WIFE, AND THE TWO SHALL BECOME ONE FLESH' ? So then, they are no longer two but one flesh. Therefore what God has joined together, let not man separate." They said to Him, "Why then did Moses command to give a certificate of divorce, and to put her away?" He said to them, "Moses, because of the hardness of your hearts, permitted you to divorce your wives, but from the beginning it was not so. And I say to you, whoever divorces his wife, except for sexual immorality, and marries another, commits adultery; and whoever marries her who is divorced commits adultery" (Matthew 19:3-9).

Here we see an account of the Pharisees approaching Jesus to ask him a question concerning divorce. We have already established that divorce is covenant breaking. Divorce is a departure from a life-long commitment. So when the Pharisees come to Jesus to ask Him about marriage and divorce, they are actually asking Him a question concerning the keeping and breaking of covenant.

They ask Jesus the question of the lawfulness of a man divorcing his wife for any reason. Is it lawful for a man to break covenant with his wife for any reason that he chooses? Jesus answers the question by referring back to the time of creation. He says, "Have you not read that He who made them at the BEGINNING made them male and female."

Jesus basically says, 'Let's start at the beginning.' We can't talk about the breaking of a covenant until we first define its composition. Jesus says that the standard for marriage is that which God created in the beginning. The standard for covenant was already established by the Father when He created man and woman.

Jesus says that the marriage covenant is between one man and one woman. GOD ESTABLISHED THAT WHICH CON-

STITUTES A MARRIAGE AT CREATION! It appears that many prominent people who are leading our nation failed to get that memo!

God Did It Right!

God did it right! God did it right when he created a man and a woman. God did it right when He put them together. God did it right when He told them to be fruitful and multiply. God did it right when He told them to have a sexual relationship and replenish the earth. God did it right.

He did not place Adam with a dog, cat, cow, horse, or any other four-footed beast. God did not create another man for Adam. He did not create Adam and Bill. He did not create Eve and Charlene. He did not create Adam, Eve, and a pornographic magazine or movie. He created one male and one female and commanded them to have a sexual relationship. Anything outside of this is perversion and sin. Anything outside of God's original design is to spit in His face. It is the ultimate demonstration of human arrogance.

I've heard people say, "Jesus never said anything about homosexuality." Unfortunately, those individuals only advertise their lack of knowledge. Jesus was very clear about homosexuality. Jesus said the Father God settled the issue at the time of creation when He created one man and one woman. No more arguments. No more discussion. Slam dunk and case is closed!

Jesus went on to say in this passage of Scripture that a MAN would leave his father and mother and be joined to his WIFE. Jesus did not say a MAN would be joined to his HUSBAND. He did not say that a WOMAN would be joined to her WIFE. Jesus specifically said that a man is to be joined to his wife, and they become one flesh. We should come into agreement with that by echoing the words of the Apostle Paul who said, "Let God be true but every man a liar" (Romans 3:4). Jesus said it, I believe it, and that settles it!

Those who lobby today for homosexual marriages have set themselves against God's original design. They have chosen to fight against that which God ordained. They have taken a position that is contradictory to that which He established at the beginning. It's as if they say, 'God, You did not know what You were doing when You made a man and a woman.' Sadly, these people have been deceived by the devil and are on the road of destruction. We don't see others in the Bible coming out victorious when they chose to fight God. Pharaoh learned this the hard way.

My friend, homosexuality is fornication. Regardless if a state or national government decides to recognize homosexual marriage, God will not change! In the Old Testament it was sin and so it is in the New.

Love Confronts

Anytime you make these kinds of truthful statements from God's Word there are accusations of being homophobic, hateful, discriminatory, or non-loving. None of these accusations are true. These accusations are hurled in an attempt to discredit truthful confrontation of sin. Vilify the messenger and the message is automatically wrong. This is the line of thinking that these accusers hold.

Understand that we can denounce the act of stealing, yet still love the thief. We can denounce the act of adultery, yet still love the adulterer. We can denounce the act of fornication, yet still love the fornicator. We can denounce the act of homosexuality, yet still love the homosexual.

In our contemporary culture today we have defined love as "say nothing about my sin, accept it, and be ok with it." This is absolutely ridiculous and incorrect. Jesus did not do that! Jesus was love manifested in the flesh and He constantly confronted sin and iniquity. Jesus told people they needed to change and turn from wickedness.

Love means that you will confront sin. Love means that you will tell your children if they are going the wrong way. Love means that you will warn someone if their life is in danger. Love compels you to tell someone if they are going the wrong direction. Love compels you to say, 'This is the way of the Lord, walk in it.'

Go and Sin No More

The fact is that Jesus died for the homosexual just like He died for the murderer. He loves them both. However, repentance from dead works and sin is a prerequisite for salvation. God has never accepted sin and never will. He has always confronted it and demanded repentance and change.

I have always been amazed at the people who quote the Scripture where the woman is caught in adultery and Jesus says, "I don't condemn you." The people who quote this Scripture the most fail to quote the remaining part of the verse. Jesus then said, "Go and sin no more." Let me paraphrase this for you, 'STOP YOUR SINNING!' Jesus confronted her sin and told her to stop it. He didn't say, 'I understand and it's all right as long as you don't get caught again, and by the way, you may want to consider another woman instead because that would be ok.'

My friend, you cannot live a life of adultery, fornication, or any other type of sexual perversion (including pornography) and experience the life of God, the ZOE of God. If you can, then Jesus lied. However, I believe that Jesus spoke the truth. He said that if you want to enter into zoe (the life of God), you must keep the commandments. That's not law, that's the truth!

Follow the Pattern

Going back to the previous passage of Scripture, Jesus uses that which the Father did at the beginning of creation as the standard. Jesus refers back to "the beginning" twice in this passage. He uses it in relationship to that which constitutes a marriage and then the command of the keeping of covenant. Jesus specifically addresses the issues of the start and continuation of covenant.

He makes this statement in His discourse, "What God has joined together, let no man separate." The Greek word translated "separate" means to go away from. Jesus says not to go away from what God put together. What did God put together? First of all, He put a man and a woman together. Jesus commanded that we stick with the pattern that God initiated at creation. We are not to go away from one man and one woman as the pattern for marriage.

This also means that once a man and woman are married they are to remain in covenant with each other. They are to stay committed. They are to remain faithful. They are not to walk away from the commitment they made to their spouse.

Again, the heart of the commandment has to do with more than just marriage. It has to do with a heart that acknowledges and follows through with covenant and commitment. I assure you that there is great blessing that God releases on those who will do this. God promises to bless those who will be faithful to their commitments.

Avoiding the Traps

I would like to go back to a previous Scripture to share some things concerning how to maintain a covenant.

If your right eye causes you to sin, pluck it out and cast it from you; for it is more profitable for you that one of your members perish, than for your whole body to be cast into hell. And if your right hand causes you to sin, cut it off and cast it from you; for it is more

*profitable for you that one of your members perish,
than for your whole body to be cast into hell"
(Matthew 5:29-30).*

I want to bring your attention to the words "causes you to sin." Jesus is referring to things that cause people to yield to temptation. He is speaking of anything within our lives that would lead us down a road of destruction. It could even be those who are negative influences in our lives.

Anything that would cause you to break covenant should be removed. If you can't watch television without tuning in to things that causes sexual desire to be illicitly stirred and your mind to wander down roads it shouldn't, then throw the television out of your house if you must. If you can't get on the internet without going to a pornographic site, then shut down the internet service and throw your computer away if need be.

If it's social media that is fostering unholy relationships and flirtatious behavior then close down your page. If you are regularly tempted to do anything unholy because of certain things that may be in your life then get rid of them. Do whatever you need to do to avoid the very appearance of evil and keep yourself out of those situations.

It's not a question as to whether the Lord has empowered us to overcome temptation. That has already been settled. The question is whether you will use and activate that power in the moment of temptation. The best thing to do is avoid situations where there is vulnerability. Many times, by making some minor changes within our lives, we can avoid the traps of sin.

My wife and I have found in many marriages where major issues existed, improvement came immediately with some minor adjustments. It's amazing how marriages can blossom when placed in the right environment and how they can wilt in the wrong one. Just slight changes can produce lasting effects.

Cut It Off

So Jesus is saying that anything which would cause you to look in the direction of sin is to be cut off and removed. He goes on to say that it is better to go through life without the thing that causes you to sin than to be cast into hell. I recognize that there may be different ways of interpreting exactly what Jesus meant when he said "hell." However, I believe that we can all agree that this is not the place we want to be.

I personally believe there are two applications of this Scripture. The **first** most literal understanding is that if you allow something to exist in your life that causes you to sin it can ultimately cause you to go to hell. I have seen good people go down the road of backsliding as a result of sin dabbling. They feel as though they can sin and not get burned. They believe that they can dabble in unholy behavior, and they are exempt from being harmed. The next thing you know they have turned their back on God, left the church, and cursed God. The end of that life is not good.

The **second** understanding is that if you allow something in your life to exist that provokes you to sin, it will cause you to experience torment while you are still alive. Sin opens the door for the devil to steal, kill, and destroy. The enemy has no point of entry in our lives unless we yield one over to him. However, many people do this regularly and then wonder why God allowed these kinds of things to happen to them. I'm convinced that we can avoid many adverse situations if we will just get rid of the things that lead us down the road of sin.

This is why Jesus, when instructing His disciples how to pray, told them to pray, "Lead us not into temptation and deliver us from evil" (Matthew 6:13). Pray that God will keep you away from that which would cause you to sin. Cut off the things within your life that are offensive through daily prayer and fellowship with God. Do whatever it takes to avoid sinful behavior.

Sin will destroy you if allowed a place of activity within your life.

When Jesus spoke this concerning removing the thing that offends and causes one to sin, He said it in relationship to lust, adultery, and divorce. He was speaking specifically in relationship to that which we have established as covenant breaking. He said it is better to remove the offensive thing than go to hell. Understand that there is no blessing surrounding the breaking of covenant.

Divorce Hurts

I have witnessed in others the fruits of divorce and can tell you that it is a very unpleasant experience. People are hurt. Husbands are hurt. Wives are hurt. Children are hurt. Relatives are hurt. The ramifications of covenant breaking are far reaching. That's the reason Jesus said to deal with the issues that would take you down the road of sin. Sin hurts and destroys.

I want to make sure that you understand that I am in no way condemning anyone who has experienced divorce. However, I would be amiss if I did not tell you that God's best is to remain married to the one with whom you made covenant. God's best is not divorce.

It's understandable when there are extreme situations of abuse within a marriage, and separation is the only option. No believer is under a requirement of remaining married where their life is in danger, or they are being battered. God does not expect any of His children to stay and suffer the fruits of stupidity from another person. Nor does he expect anyone to stay when the offending spouse is repeatedly committing acts of sexual perversion within the household or outside the household.

Hard-Heartedness

Jesus expressly said that divorce was instituted because of hard-heartedness. Covenant breaking is the result of a heart that has hardened. We see it manifesting through pride in the offending party. Self-justification is another manifestation of a heart that is hardened. Understand that sin will cause one's heart to become calloused. It can cause a person to become unfeeling toward others that they are hurting. They will take no thought of anything they do regardless of who they hurt. When hearts become hard, divorce is the result.

We also see hard-heartedness manifesting in the way of inability to forgive. Holding on to an offense and rehearsing it will cause a heart to become bitter. I believe that forgiveness is a better solution than divorce. In other words, cut off the offense you are holding on to rather than go through the traumatic experience of divorce. If at all possible, walk down the road of forgiveness rather than the road of divorce.

There are many other Scriptures throughout the New Testament that we could share on covenant breaking. Needless to say, God frowns on it. It was wrong in the Old Testament and it's wrong in the New Testament. Jesus and the Apostle Paul reinforce the seventh commandment. The heart of the commandment is to maintain covenant and commitment.

Broken covenants produce broken people. Shattered commitments shatter people. Hurt and pain are the result of these things. If we will choose to obey this commandment, we will avoid the pain and heartache. If we will heed the words of Jesus, we can experience His life.

Life Released Where Unity Exists

The Psalmist David said this:

A Song of Ascents. Of David. Behold, how good and how pleasant it is For brethren to dwell together in unity! It is like the precious oil upon the head, Running down on the beard, The beard of Aaron, Running down on the edge of his garments. It is like the dew of Hermon, Descending upon the mountains of Zion; For there the LORD commanded the blessing— Life forevermore (Psalm 133:1-3).

I want you to notice the last verse of this psalm: "For there the Lord commanded the blessing, life forevermore." Where does God command the blessing? It is the place where people are in unity. It is the place where there is the absence of separation. It is the place where people are dwelling together, not merely tolerating one another.

The Lord says that "life forevermore" is the result of unity. Likewise, Jesus said that life (*zoe*) is the byproduct of keeping the commandments. This includes the command of maintaining covenant and commitment. So as we continue in covenant we bring forth the fruit of unity which results in life. I trust you see the connection.

These Scriptures can be applied to our marriages and homes. We can and will experience the anointing of the Holy Spirit as we maintain covenant. We will see refreshing come as we follow through with our commitments to one another. We will see life forevermore as we are faithful in covenant.

Please pray this prayer with me:

Father God, I make a fresh commitment today to follow Your command to not commit adultery. I appropriate forgiveness for any place within my life where I have broken this com-

mand. I receive deliverance and healing as I renounce the hidden works of darkness.

Today, I forsake any and all types of sexual perversion. I choose to follow You, Lord. I choose to be faithful to the covenants and commitments I have made. Thank You for Your grace that empowers and enables me to fulfill Your commandment. Thank You for power and ability to live above sin. Sin will not have dominion over me. In Jesus name. Amen.

CHAPTER TEN
GIVERS AND TAKERS

"You shall not steal."
(Exodus 20:15)

Once again a simple command is stated: do not steal. Do not take that which belongs to someone else. If you don't own it, don't take it. I think it's so interesting that many of these commands that are articulated within the Ten Commandments are not complicated. God does not make it difficult to understand. Four simple words are stated here.

No Exceptions

The first word is the word that is most difficult for many to hear. That is the word "YOU." The word "you" indicates that God is talking to each of us individually. The word "you" denotes that none of us are the exception.

It is amazing how some people choose to make themselves the exception through human reasoning. If you are looking for justification to do wrong, I am sure you will find it. However, it requires one to exempt themselves from the command they are breaking. The word "you" says there are no exemptions.

One translation of this verse reads, "Do not take the property of another." I believe it is very clear that God detests thievery. The word "steal" literally means to thieve. God commands His people to refrain from being thieves.

In John 10:10, Jesus spoke of what He came to do versus what the thief comes to do. He said, "The thief does not come except to steal, and to kill, and to destroy. I have come that they might have life, and that they may have it more abundantly." Many great preachers have taught from this Scripture that the devil is the thief. Could it be that God does not want us to steal because it emulates the behavior of the devil? Could it be that if we steal we look like Satan? Think about it.

Live As a Giver

Now once again, grace does not abolish the command. Grace raises the bar. It elevates the standard. It empowers us to fulfill the letter of the law and the spirit of the command. It enables us to achieve the heart of Father when the command was given.

I believe the heart of the Father contained within this commandment is to live your life as a giver and not a taker. There are primarily two kinds of people in the world today. There are those who live as givers, and there are those who live as takers. The givers live with an open hand. The takers live with a closed fist.

The reality of living your life as a giver will prevent you from becoming a thief. It prevents you from stealing. It keeps you from taking that which doesn't belong to you. Those who live their lives as takers are the ones who end up falling short of the requirement of this commandment.

Jesus had a lot to say about giving. He had a lot to say about the lifestyle of a giver. He taught us to live to give and be a blessing to others.

"Give, and it will be given to you: good measure, pressed down, shaken together, and running over will be put into your bosom. For with the same measure that you use, it will be measured back to you." (Luke 6:38).

Giving Is the Heart of the Father

Understand again, Jesus takes every commandment to the next level. I think it's important to note that in the Sermon on the Mount, Jesus addresses most all of the Ten Commandments either directly or indirectly. He reinforces them and explains the heart of the Father. He reveals a deeper understanding as He expounds on the spirit of the law.

In the Old Testament the command was don't take that which is not yours. Jesus now takes it a step further and says "GIVE." In a preceding verse, He actually says to give to those who ask and lend expecting nothing in return. You cannot do this unless you have transitioned from the life of a taker to the life of a giver.

We are not born into this world as givers; we are born takers. That's the reason we must be born again. It is not within the fleshly nature of a human to be a giver. We need a new nature and our minds renewed to become givers. We receive a new nature when we are born of the Spirit.

Babies cry because they want someone to give them something. As they grow up and begin to play with each other, sharing is not a natural trait which they already possess. Taking another child's toy is something that comes rather natural. They must be taught to share. Giving is something that humans must be taught to do. Even Christians must be taught to be givers.

Jesus Is a Giver

Jesus was all about giving. He taught others to GIVE. He came to GIVE His life a ransom for many. He came to GIVE us abundant life. He came to GIVE us mercy, love, and grace. Everything Jesus did was motivated from a heart of giving. Jesus was not a taker. He did not come to the earth to see what He could get.

Living your life as a taker is to live your life as a thief. That is what thieves do. They live in an opportunistic manner looking for someone they can "rip-off." They are only concerned with themselves and their desires. It doesn't matter to them if someone else is hurt as a result of their action. As far as they are concerned, that which you own is only there so they can take it. What a miserable existence this is.

God did not create us to live in this manner. He created you and me so we could be a blessing to others. He ordained that we emulate His nature which is to give. God is a giver.

Arguably the most well-known Scripture in the Bible is John 3:16. It declares, "God so loved the world that He gave His only begotten Son." Notice that He GAVE. Love compelled Him to give. Think about this. God loved you and me so much that He chose to GIVE. He wasn't required; He chose to give.

You can tell if someone is walking in love by the manner in which they give. You can give without loving, but you cannot love without giving. Love will always require you to give. It will motivate and induce giving within your life.

You Owe Me

There are many people today that live with a "you owe me" attitude. Their thinking is that they have been victimized by others and now the whole world owes them. This type of thinking leads down a path which ends with them becoming takers rather than givers. I have yet to see anyone with the "you owe me" attitude live as a giver. They are usually bitter, mad at the world, and consumed with themselves. This is not the way that God desires us to live. However, this is the result of those who choose to live their lives as takers. Why live in this manner needlessly? You can live your life as a giver.

If you have been living with the "you owe me" attitude, I encourage you to get rid of it quickly. That disposition is paralyzing. It will cause you to feel spiteful at anyone who has something that you don't. It ultimately leads to the breaking of another command which is "do not covet." None of us can afford to live with that type of attitude. My friend, if that is your outlook on life, you will suffer. You will miss out on the joy and the blessing of giving.

The Blessing of Giving

Jesus said, "It is more blessed to give than to receive" (Acts 20:25). He said that giving is better than receiving. There is joy in giving. There is blessing in living as a giver. Let me say this verse in another way. There is greater blessing living as a giver rather than a taker!

Jesus emphasized the importance of giving. He stated that the blessing is on the giving side as opposed to the receiving side. I believe we can get to a place within our lives where we are more excited about giving than receiving. We can arrive at a point to where we take greater joy in giving to others than receiving from others.

None of us should live with the purpose of seeing how much we can get. This is not the goal of life. The legacy and testimony that I desire to leave is that I was a generous man. That only happens as the result of living as a giver. How horrible is it to have the reputation of being stingy? Yet, if you live as a taker, that will be the end result. No one wants to be around stingy people. That attitude pervades in everything they do. They are always looking for that which they can get rather than what they can give.

Isaiah 32:8 declares, "A generous man devises generous things, and by generosity he shall stand." Being generous will cause you to stand in times of adversity. Being a giver will produce the blessing of God within your life. That's what I want. How about you? Choose to live as a giver.

Labor to Give

"Let him who stole steal no longer, but rather let him labor, working with his hands what is good, that he may have something to give him who has need" (Ephesians 4:28).

Paul says several things in this verse to which I want to draw your attention. The first thing is that Paul reemphasizes the commandment of "you shall not steal." He says to stop stealing. In the New Testament, stealing is forbidden. Just as it was in the Old Testament, so it is in the New. It hasn't changed. It is only rearticulated.

Paul goes on to state the solution to stealing. He says, "Let him labor, working...that he may have something to give." If you were to ask most people today the question of why they go to work every day, they would respond with the answer, "To make a living." It seems that for most people the idea of labor and work is solely for the purpose of their own provision. However, Paul says something different. He says the purpose of work and labor is so one can be a giver. Paul takes the purpose of work beyond the concept of personal provision. This is a radical idea in the minds of most people today.

It's very interesting how Paul contrasts stealing with giving. This only emphasizes that the heart of the eighth commandment is to live as a giver. Paul states the necessity of working is not based upon the need to accumulate. He says that labor is essential for the purpose of giving.

Laziness Produces Thievery

People who are unwilling to work are usually the ones who live their lives as takers. They live their lives as thieves. When someone refuses to be productive while expecting everyone else to provide for them, they are thieves. Nobody owes you or me a living because we're breathing. The bottom line is Paul commands the Christians at Ephesus to get a job and work. He told them to stop living as thieves and start living as givers.

I recognize there are some who are unfortunate. I also recognize there are some who cannot work for various health related reasons. However, if you can work, get a job. Paul said that if a man doesn't work, then he shouldn't eat. The prerequisite for having provision is working and laboring.

Jesus never excused us from being diligent and productive. He never commanded us to refrain from labor and allow Him to bring money to our mailbox. Jesus shared parables that involved commendation of the faithful servant who was productive and condemnation of the lazy servant who hid his talent. Jesus went so far as to say the lazy servant was wicked (Matthew 25:26). At no time did Jesus ever encourage laziness.

When God created man, He placed him in the Garden of Eden. God planted a garden and told Adam to tend to it. This meant he would be required to work. The garden was not a

NEXT LEVEL—Raising the Standard of Grace

place of eternal vacation. Even though it was a place of perfection, work was still mandated by God.

Again, Paul states that a man is to labor that he may have something to give. Two specific directives are given in this verse: work and give. Hence, we see the true purpose for God's blessing that is produced through our labor and diligence. It is so that we will have something to give. We are to live our lives as givers.

God Doesn't Change

"For I am the LORD, I do not change; Therefore you are not consumed, O sons of Jacob. Yet from the days of your fathers You have gone away from My ordinances And have not kept them. Return to Me, and I will return to you," Says the LORD of hosts. "But you said, 'In what way shall we return?' Will a man rob God? Yet you have robbed Me! But you say, 'In what way have we robbed You?' In tithes and offerings. You are cursed with a curse, For you have robbed Me, Even this whole nation. Bring all the tithes into the storehouse, That there may be food in My house, And try Me now in this," Says the LORD of hosts, "If I will not open for you the windows of heaven And pour out for you such blessing That there will not be room enough to receive it. And I will rebuke the devourer for your sakes, So that he will not destroy the fruit of your ground, Nor shall the vine fail to bear fruit for you in the field," Says the LORD of hosts; "And all nations will call you blessed, For you will be a delightful land," Says the LORD of hosts (Malachi 3:6-12).

I love this passage of Scripture. It is filled with the promise of God. It guarantees God's provision in our lives. These verses of Scripture assure us of the Father's desire and plan to bless us. Anyone who reads this passage of Scripture should be thrilled and excited.

138

There are numerous things that I want to point out. However, the first thing I want to draw your attention to is what many Christians miss. It is found in verse six. The Lord says, "For I am the Lord, I do not change." God desires for His people to know that He is the same yesterday, today, and forever.

Understand that there is not an Old Testament God and a New Testament God. He is the same. He does not change. His principles do not change. They have always been and will always be. The process of redemption and dealing with sin changed from the Old to the New. However, God did not change, nor did His kingdom principles.

So before the Lord begins a discourse on tithes and offerings, He precipitates it with the statement of "I'm not changing." By doing this He indicates that the principle of the tithe is not going to change. This is the only time in the Bible where God specifically says, "I do not change." It's located immediately before a discourse on tithes and offerings. Do you think that God was attempting to communicate something to His people? I think so.

I have heard some people say that tithing is only applicable in the Old Testament. Likewise, some of these same people say the Ten Commandments are not applicable for us under the New Covenant. They go on to say that tithing is not required in the New Covenant. My response to them is that tithing is neither Old nor New Testament. It is a kingdom principle that began before the Old Covenant was established. Abraham tithed before the Law was established and before any commandment was given. However, tithing is rearticulated and demonstrated in both the Old and New Testaments.

There are a tremendous amount of books and teaching material on the biblical importance of the tithe. I will not take time to go into great depth on this subject. Just suffice to say that tithing is required of us in the New Testament just as it was in the Old Testament because it transcends both covenants. It is a kingdom principle that was enacted by an unchangeable God.

Tither or Thief?

Looking at verse eight of this passage in Malachi, God asks an unusual question. It is a question that does not seem feasible. He asks, "Will a man rob (steal from) God?" Then He makes sure that they know they have stolen from Him. God knew the people would ask, "How have we robbed (stolen from) You?" He gives them the answer, "In tithes and offerings." Then He issues a command to bring all the tithes and offering to the storehouse.

Once again this ties back to the heart of the commandment of "you will not steal." God declared that His people were stealing from Him. They had withheld the tithe and the offering. They were not living as givers; they were living as takers. They had taken that to which God had already laid claim.

The tithe belongs to the Lord. It does not belong to us. The first ten percent of our income is not ours; it belongs to the Lord. If we take that ten percent, we are stealing. We are taking something that belongs to someone else. That someone else is God Almighty.

It always amazes me that those who want God to do everything for them are usually the ones who give little to nothing. They live their lives as takers. They are willing to take anything and everything the Lord and anyone else will give them. However, they are unwilling to tithe, give offerings, or anything that may require something of them. They usually live on a spiritual merry-go-round where they continue to encounter the same issues. They wonder why nothing is working for them while they continue to live in a disobedient manner. If this is you, CHANGE! I encourage you to do it quickly.

God wanted to bless His people. He wanted to pour out abundant provision. However, He couldn't. Why? It was because they were living their lives as takers rather than givers. They were stealing from Him. They were thieves. They were breaking the commandment of "you will not steal." The failure to tithe is the breaking of the eighth commandment.

Forsaking thievery is not an option in the life of a believer. Neither is tithing an option. This is a command that is not up for debate. It is not a command where one can "opt out." Believers who fail to tithe forsake the blessing of God that has been promised to them. They set themselves up for the curse to be manifested. My friend, it's not worth it.

Faith in God or a Stolen Tithe?

I've told the people in our church that failure to tithe is putting your faith and confidence in the ten percent that doesn't belong to you. It doesn't make sense that someone would do that. Why would someone put their confidence in ten percent that was stolen? If you are caught with stolen goods, you go to jail. If you steal something and it is found out, you go to jail. Why put your faith in that which may send you to jail? Think about it.

Many people think they can live their lives in this manner and there will be no consequences. That is simply not true. God said to the people who were stealing from Him that they were cursed. Disobedience doesn't pay. Let me say it in a way that you may understand better. Crime doesn't pay.

Someone once said, "I can't afford to tithe." My friend, we can't afford to stop tithing. Why would I want to curse myself by withholding the tithe? Why would I want to cut off my blessing through hanging on to that which does not belong to me? For what good reason could I ever steal from God after all He's done for me? That's called shooting yourself in the foot. That's called jumping out of the frying pan and into the fire.

Most people who have heard teaching on the tithe, yet refuse to do so, will have some type of justification for their neglect. I've heard them all. But those excuses will never make the lifestyle of a taker justifiable. Our human reasoning will not change God's command for our lives.

A Second Chance

The wonderful thing about the Lord is that He is redemptive in nature. He gives His people an opportunity to make things right. In Malachi, God challenges them to prove Him. He admonishes them to stop stealing and start bringing the tithe and offering to the storehouse, and He will open the windows of heaven and pour out great blessing. He challenges them to be givers rather than takers.

There is great blessing that God has reserved for the giver. In the Scripture we shared earlier, Jesus said that as we give, it would be given to us in an overflowing manner. That's what I want for my life. I want the overflow. Jesus promised that givers will live in that overflowing manner and be blessed abundantly.

Jesus Reinforces the Command and the Tithe

"But woe to you Pharisees! For you tithe mint and rue and all manner of herbs, and pass by justice and the love of God. These you ought to have done, without leaving the others undone" (Luke 11:42).

Jesus reinforces the principle of the tithe and at the same time reinforces the eighth commandment. He tells the Pharisees that they are supposed to tithe. "These you ought to have done" is what He said. He was referring to tithing. Jesus was saying that we ought to live as givers.

It is important to obey the commandment of "you will not steal." It is a command that is reinforced and rearticulated in the New Testament. We must learn to live as givers rather than takers. God has promised that there will be great blessing released in our lives as we live with the disposition of a giver.

The Cheerful Giver

So let each one give as he purposes in his heart, not grudgingly or of necessity; for God loves a cheerful giver. And God is able to make all grace abound toward you, that you, always having all sufficiency in all things, may have an abundance for every good work (2 Corinthians 9:7-8).

Paul said that God loves a cheerful giver, not a cheerful taker. Grace is given to the cheerful giver. Sufficiency is released in the life of the cheerful giver. The life of the cheerful giver partakes in abundance.

The Greek word translated "cheerful" in this Scripture is *hilaros*. It is where we derive our English word "hilarious." God loves for someone to give in a hilarious manner. His desire is that we give joyfully knowing that He will bless us abundantly.

When Paul said that the giver would have all sufficiency of all things, he was saying that cheerful givers will have more than enough. That means *El-Shaddai*, the God who is more than enough, will manifest Himself on their behalf. That means *Jehovah Jireh* will be there to see that their need is supplied. That's the crowd I want to be with—the more than enough crowd! That's the cheerful giver crowd.

The letter of the law is "do not steal." The heart of the commandment is live as a giver. Grace then empowers us to give cheerfully. I trust you see the progression. We are not giving because we are merely required. We give because we want to and find joy in doing so. We live our lives as givers. As a result of that, God gives back to us in an overwhelming manner. Hallelujah!

I encourage you to refuse to live your life as a taker. Choose to live as a giver. You will be glad you did.

Please pray this prayer with me:

Father God, I make a fresh commitment today to follow Your command to not steal. I appropriate forgiveness for any place within my life where I have broken this command. I receive deliverance and healing as I renounce the hidden works of darkness.

Today, I forsake any and all types of thievery and robbery. I choose to follow You, Lord. I choose to live my life as a giver rather than a taker. Thank You for Your grace that empowers and enables me to fulfill Your commandment. Thank You, Holy Spirit, for Your ability to live above sin. Sin will not have dominion over me. In the name of Jesus, I pray. Amen.

CHAPTER ELEVEN

SPEAK THE TRUTH

"You shall not bear false witness against your neighbor."
Exodus 20:16

The ninth commandment explicitly forbids lying about anyone. Under the law, no one was allowed to bring an untruthful testimony against another person. The reason for this command is that one could be prosecuted and convicted unjustly if they were to do so. God strictly forbids anyone from doing such a thing to another individual.

Wesley's commentary on this commandment is this:

This forbids, speaking falsely in any matter, lying, equivocating, and any way devising and designing to deceive our neighbour. Speaking unjustly against our neighbour, to the prejudice of his reputation; And (which is the highest offence of both these kinds put together) Bearing false witness against him, laying to his charge things that he knows not, either upon oath, by which the third commandment, the sixth or eighth, as well as this, are broken, or in common converse, slandering, backbiting, tale-bearing, aggravating what is done amiss, and any way endeavouring to raise our own reputation upon the ruin of our neighbor's.[1]

From this commentary we can see how that the result of lying is more than just the breaking of the ninth commandment. It begins to overlap in the breaking of other commandments. Lying produces an evil snowball of activity that only brings destruction, heartache, and pain.

Why People Lie

Before I get into the spirit and heart of this commandment, I would like to expose some of the reasons that people lie. The majority of time, someone who speaks untruthfully about another individual does not do so merely for the reason of dislike. It is usually not for the reason of causeless aversion. Rarely does someone wake up one morning, decide they loathe someone for no reason, and then bring a false accusation against that person. Only in extreme cases does that happen, but that is not the norm.

There are, what I consider, three primary reasons that people lie. The **first** is to protect themselves or someone else. It is rooted in the fear of a negative consequence if the truth were known. It is also called "cover up." People will lie to protect. When the truth is hidden, a lie is propagated. We see this in many areas of our society and culture today. We read and hear about cover ups to repress the truth. This is wrong.

The **second** reason is to gain an advantage over someone else. Those who engage in this type of behavior believe their cause can be advanced by defaming another. They seek to advance their own agenda through the unjust and untrue accusations that damage the reputation of another individual. How often have we seen this in the political arena? It's more than I can count or enumerate. The philosophy is if people hear something enough they will believe it, whether true or false. This is manipulative behavior that only seeks to exalt self.

The **third** reason is for the purpose of retaliation. Someone becomes angry at another so they hurl false accusations in an attempt to hurt the other individual. Sometimes, the person who is the false accuser may have been genuinely hurt by the person they are accusing. However, two wrongs do not make a right.

So, we see the three primary reasons are protection, gain an advantage, and retaliation. At the end of the day, it's all sin. It's all motivated by the exaltation of self. It is the work of the flesh. Lying is never righteous and is always wrong. We will come back and discuss these reasons later.

Jesus Reveals the Heart of the Commandment

"Again you have heard that it was said to those of old, 'You shall not swear falsely, but shall perform your oaths to the Lord.' But I say to you, do not swear at all: neither by heaven, for it is God's throne; nor by the earth, for it is His footstool; nor by Jerusalem, for it is the city of the great King. Nor shall you swear by your head, because you cannot make one hair white or black. But let your 'Yes' be 'Yes,' and your 'No,' 'No.' For whatever is more than these is from the evil one" (Matthew 5:33-37).

Once again we see that Jesus reinforces the Ten Commandments and their relevance for us in the New Testament. He gives greater understanding of the ninth commandment in His discourse in this passage of Scripture. Jesus takes the commandments to the next level. He takes it beyond the letter of the law to the heart of the commandment. To really understand what Jesus is saying, you need a little historical understanding.

The Jews had come to a place where they believed that one could say something with their mouth, but disavow it in their heart. They believed that this was acceptable. By disavowing something in their heart, lying had become in some way virtuous. Adam Clarke says in his commentary, "The morality of the Jews on this point was truly execrable: they maintained, that a man might swear with his lips, and annul it in the same moment in his heart."[2]

It is apparent that lying had become the practice of the day. Perjury was commonplace. To validate their lies, they would swear in the name of the Lord knowing they were lying the entire time. This means they were not only breaking the commandment of not bearing false witness, but were simultaneously taking the name of the Lord in vain. When they didn't swear in the name of the Lord, they would swear by other things.

Jesus tells them, "Stop swearing and stop lying." When he said "do not swear at all," you must go back to the previous verse to fully understand what He's talking about. He is referring to false swearing: lying and perjury. Jesus was declaring that swearing by the name of the Lord or any other thing does not make their words true. He tells them to stop their lying!

Jesus goes on to say, "Let your 'yes' be 'yes' and your 'no' be 'no'." Paraphrased, Jesus said, "Tell the truth." How simple is that? Just speak the truth. Do not take an oath in an attempt to validate and legitimize a lie. Just tell the truth.

Speak the Truth

Herein lays the heart of the ninth commandment. That is SPEAK THE TRUTH. Jesus said that those in covenant with God should only speak that which is truthful. He inferred that the reputation of His people should be that they simply tell the truth and that there is no need for them to take any kind of oath.

It's interesting that Jesus goes on to say that whatever goes beyond "yes" and "no" comes from the devil. He was addressing this belief that had crept into the Jews that you could swear something verbally, but disavow it in your heart at the same time; the belief that lying was permissible. Jesus said all of these things they were doing in the way of false swearing and the taking of oaths was of the devil. Why? It is because the DEVIL IS A LIAR (John 8:44). Jesus was basically telling them "You are acting like the devil, so stop it."

Contrary to popular belief, Jesus confronted sin. Most people in the church now would say that Jesus was condemning if He were to preach in their church today. Jesus didn't play around. He wasn't trying to win friends by refraining from confrontation. Jesus was in your face. He was love, yet He was in your face. Why do you think the Scribes and Pharisees hated Him? It was because Jesus constantly confronted them and called out their sin. Why do you think Herod had John the Baptist killed? It was because John confronted Herod's sin and adultery.

Somewhere along the way the church has lost its message of confrontation. When is the last time you heard the word "repent" come out of the pulpit? When is the last time you heard someone preach on the dangers of sin? Jesus preached it. Paul preached it. Why have many pastors and preachers forsaken it?

The letter of the law commanded that there be no false testimony concerning anyone else. The spirit of the command is to speak the truth all the time. Let's see what the Apostle Paul had to say:

> Therefore, putting away lying, "LET EACH ONE OF YOU SPEAK TRUTH WITH HIS NEIGHBOR," for we are members of one another. "BE ANGRY, AND DO NOT SIN": do not let the sun go down on your wrath, nor give place to the devil. Let him who stole steal no longer, but rather let him labor, working with his hands what is good, that he may have something to give him who has need. Let no corrupt word proceed out of your mouth, but what is good for necessary edification, that it may impart grace to the hearers (Ephesians 4:25-29).

Paul Reinforces the Commandment

In this passage of Scripture, Paul reinforces the commandment of "do not bear false witness." We also understand this as: "do not lie." Paul specifically says, "Put away lying." Let me translate that for you. STOP LYING! Paul is restating the ninth commandment. As we have stated throughout this book, each of the Ten Commandments are reaffirmed within the New Testament either by direct quote or the spirit of the commandment. The New Covenant did not abolish the Ten Commandments.

We can observe at least three of the Ten Commandments stated in this passage of Scripture. We see "do not bear false witness" when Paul tells them to stop lying. We see "do not murder" when he tells them to refrain from being angry. We see "do not steal" when he tells them to steal no longer. These are ones that are directly restated while others could be inferred. Grace did not abolish the Ten Commandments.

Lying Hurts Everybody

Paul says that we are to obey the ninth commandment. He says stop lying and speak the truth. We see the spirit of the command articulated by Paul when he says, "Speak truth." He then declares the purpose for ceasing lying and speaking the truth when he says, "For we are members of one another."

Paul was stating that lying hurts the body of Christ and thus hurts you. Speaking falsely about another Christian is not only harmful to them, but it is harmful to the one who is guilty of the offense. Using our tongue to tear down another person hurts everybody. If we lie about another member of the church we actually hurt ourselves.

When writing to the church at Corinth, Paul stated that when one member suffers, we all suffer. Taking that same principle we could say this: when one member has a lie spoken against them, we all suffer from it. When one member is being maligned, everyone is harmed.

I can recall many years ago, there was feuding that began to take place within the body of Christ among several prominent ministers of the day. It was on television, radio, newspapers, and magazines. Some even referred to it as "Holy Wars." Unfortunately, it reflected poorly on the entire body of Christ. I only share this to bare the point of what is being said. When accusations are being hurled at others in the body of Christ, no one is benefited.

Our tongues are to be used to bless one another. Our tongues are to be used to build up one another. Our tongues are not for the purpose of destroying others in the body of Christ. Our tongues should be agents of life rather than agents of destruction. Notwithstanding, we should still confront with the truth.

Truth and Love

"But, speaking the truth in love, may grow up in all things into Him who is the head—Christ—" (Ephesians 4:15).

Here is a general rule to go by. If it's not TRUE and if it's not LOVE, then don't say it. Speaking things other than truth and love will stunt one's growth. It prevents one from becoming that which God has called them to be. It hinders one's spiritual maturity and purpose in God. It hurts others and themselves.

Paul states that speaking things that are truthful and lovely causes us to grow up. On the other hand, lying and malicious speech will stunt one's spiritual growth. You actually hurt yourself if you lie about someone else. You actually prevent your own growth if you become verbally malicious toward another person.

No one should use their tongue to maliciously hurt someone else. Our tongue should be an agent of life, edification, and encouragement. It is not to be used as a weapon against another member of the body of Christ.

In the fourth chapter of Ephesians, Paul states twice that we are to speak the truth. Then in verse twenty-nine he says that we are to "let no corrupt communication come out of our mouth." This connects with the other verses that say we are to tell the truth. The words "corrupt communication" literally mean "worthless rotten speech."

The fact is that lying and malicious talk are worthless. They have no value. Why? It is because it devalues the person that is being maligned and the person making the untruthful statements. No one is going to think more highly about the individual making false accusations. It will actually devalue them in the eyes of those who hear the falsehoods. It will produce mistrust within the ears of those who hear the lies.

Spiritual Cannibalism

"For all the law is fulfilled in one word, even in this: 'YOU SHALL LOVE YOUR NEIGHBOR AS YOURSELF.' But if you bite and devour one another, beware lest you be consumed by one another!" (Galatians 5:14-15).

In this passage of Scripture, I want to point out the connection that Paul makes between fulfilling the law (the Ten Commandments) and malicious behavior. He states that loving your neighbor causes one to fulfill the law. If one walks in love, then the commandments will be fulfilled. He did not say the commandments were irrelevant, but that they would be obeyed as we walk in love.

Paul then contrasts love and obedience to the Ten Commandments with biting and devouring one another. What was he talking about? He was referring to believers using their tongues to destroy each other through worthless rotten speech. Lying and malicious talk is likened to spiritual cannibalism. The result of lying is equivalent to cannibalism.

That's absolutely gross to consider. If it's gross to think about, then we could conclude that God gets "grossed out" at this type of behavior in the body of Christ. It is repulsive and it's time to stop it. Lying hurts the church. Lying and malicious talk damages everyone. The bottom line is if you can't say something good about someone then be quiet.

We need to understand that the ninth commandment deals with both the proper and improper use of our tongues. God's design for that member of our body was to be used as an agent of life and blessing. However, many have used it as an agent of death and destruction.

> But no man can tame the tongue. It is an unruly evil, full of deadly poison. With it we bless our God and

Father, and with it we curse men, who have been made in the similitude of God. Out of the same mouth proceed blessing and cursing. My brethren, these things ought not to be so. Does a spring send forth fresh water and bitter from the same opening? Can a fig tree, my brethren, bear olives, or a grapevine bear figs? Thus no spring yields both salt water and fresh. Who is wise and understanding among you? Let him show by good conduct that his works are done in the meekness of wisdom. But if you have bitter envy and self-seeking in your hearts, do not boast and lie against the truth (James 3:8-14).

James talks about the tongue and its use in blessing and cursing. He says that it's not right for us to bless God and curse men. He declares, "These things ought not to be so." He was actually saying, 'Stop it.' I think the most interesting thing in this Scripture passage is found in verse fourteen when James says, "Do not boast and lie against the truth."

In essence, what James is saying is that if someone uses their tongue to curse or malign someone else, they are in actuality lying against the truth. Wow! Think about it! Speaking evil of our brother is equivocated to lying. We break the ninth commandment if we use our tongue to curse others.

I recognize that we all have probably fallen short in this area at some point within our lives. Probably every Christian has allowed some type of corrupt communication to come out of their mouths at an unguarded moment. So this is not meant to condemn; it is meant to illuminate. It is important that we see that our tongue is to be used properly and that it is sinful if we maliciously speak or lie about someone.

The Power of the Tongue

Proverbs says, "Death and life are in the power of the tongue" (Proverbs 18:21). That which we speak determines whether it is one or the other. James encourages believers to bless God and bless others with the words of their mouths. When we do this, life is released. Not only in the lives of others, but it's released within our lives, too.

Over the last five years or so, social networking has become very popular. Hardly anyone who has access to the internet doesn't have a social network page. As a result, a forum has been created that allows for anyone to say anything to anybody about any other individual. Things are said and propagated that should not be said. Since there are very few parameters concerning what can be said through postings, we have a plethora of stuff that is meaningless and "worthless rotten speech."

It brings no edification. It does not bless. Sometimes it can be filled with vulgarity and inappropriate material. Much of it is self-exalting and condescending to others. I have come to the conclusion that if James were alive today, he would be saying, 'Out of the same computer (and/or smart phone or tablet) proceed blessing and cursing...these things ought not to be so."

The fact that anyone who has nothing good to say can publish their foolishness in less than a minute has brought new definition to the word "insanity." There was a day when the ignorance of the foolish was not celebrated. However, we are in a different age where discernment is lacking and wisdom is scarce. As a result, people post things that are untruthful and others believe it solely because it sounds believable.

At the end of the day people are hurt as lies are propagated. Others are deceived as they believe things that are untrue. Here is a bit of wisdom. Just because it's posted on the internet does not mean it's true. Just because someone has a title before or after their name does not mean that it is accurate or that it is credible. The internet and social networking has allowed the opportunity for the proliferation of lies and un-truths. It has given those who regularly malign others increased ability to harm.

Understand that the internet and social networking are not the villains in and of themselves. It has just aided and plat-formed that which is in the heart of men and women. Notice what Jesus says:

> *"Do you not yet understand that whatever enters the mouth goes into the stomach and is eliminated? But those things which proceed out of the mouth come from the heart, and they defile a man. For out of the heart proceed evil thoughts, murders, adulteries, forni-cations, thefts, false witness, blasphemies. These are the things which defile a man, but to eat with un-washed hands does not defile a man" (Matthew 15:17-20).*

Defiled by Your Own Words

In the above verses, Jesus is explaining His response to the scribes and Pharisees concerning their accusatory question of why His disciples ate with unwashed hands and transgressed the tradition of the elders. When you read the entire chapter you can recognize that Jesus was rather perturbed at these reli-gious leaders. They could never see the forest for the trees. They were so focused on one thing that they could never get the big picture and see the heart of the Father.

Jesus explains later to His disciples that it is not what enters into the mouth of a man that has the ability to defile him. It is that which goes out of his mouth that has opportunity to defile. Jesus also makes a connection between the heart and the mouth. He says that which goes out of the mouth comes from the heart. He then enunciates the different things that can proceed from the heart that is articulated with the mouth. One of those things is false witness or lying.

Jesus says that lying will defile a man. The Greek word that is translated "defile" means to make profane, unclean, and pollute. Lying will pollute you. It will make you unclean. Evil speaking will make you profane. That is what Jesus said.

My friend, I don't want to have any of these meanings of defile within my life. I do not want to be unclean, polluted, or profane. However, if one chooses to speak lies, untruths, or malicious words, they will be defiled according to Jesus.

In the very beginning of this chapter we briefly discussed three primary reasons people lie. They were to protect, gain advantage, and retaliation. It is recognizable that people who slander someone else will usually do this for one of the reasons stated above. Someone who maliciously uses their tongue to malign another will do it for one of these three reasons stated. Again, people do not wake up one day and just have a vendetta against someone else. They are usually trying to protect themselves, gain an advantage, or retaliate.

Motive That Justifies—The Vicious Circle

We are talking about motive—that which motivates someone to do something. Understand that motive is what proceeds from the heart. This is why Jesus talks about that which proceeds from a man's heart resulting in words coming out of their mouth. The motive of the heart determines what comes out of the mouth. We could also say that the motive of the heart determines that which gets posted on the internet and social networks.

Herein we can observe the deceptiveness of lying. Those who lie feel they have justification. They have a reason and justifiable motive in their own mind even though this is the primary lie. The lie that they believe concerning their justification is greater than the one that proceeds out of their mouth. It becomes a vicious circle. The lie someone believes concerning justification of sin causes them to lie which then defiles and pollutes them with more untruths.

These people live on Satan's merry-go-round as they use their tongue to lie and malign. They come to the point where they believe their own lie. It is a great place of danger when a lie one speaks sounds like the truth to them. The end result is not good.

I have known of people who have lied to such a degree that they actually have convinced themselves it is the truth. This will never happen to those who refuse to give themselves over to lying, backbiting, slander, and malicious talk. Ask the Lord to put a watch over your mouth so that no corrupt word would come out of it.

Stop Lying and Experience Life

"For 'HE WHO WOULD LOVE LIFE AND SEE GOOD DAYS, LET HIM REFRAIN HIS TONGUE FROM EVIL, AND HIS LIPS FROM SPEAKING DECEIT'" (1 Peter 3:10).

Peter quotes a passage of Scripture located in Psalm 34. He says that if you want life, then refrain from speaking deceit. The word that was originally used in the Hebrew language for "deceit" means deceiving, fraud, or false. Peter is saying if one wants to experience life (*zoe*), he must refrain from lying.

This sounds like what Jesus said. The rich young ruler came to Jesus asking the question of what he needed to do to inherit life (*zoe*). Jesus told him, "Keep the commandments." One of the commandments that Jesus specifically mentioned was to "not bear false witness." Here, Peter says the same thing. If you want to experience the life of God then you must refrain from lying. Keep your tongue from speaking evil, deception, and falsehood. Speak the truth in love.

The Need for Wisdom

I understand that there are times that unpleasant things have to be addressed and discussed. Leaders of churches and ministries recognize that there are some things that happen that require total disclosure and transparency. However, we must use wisdom and discernment to determine what, when, where, and with whom those issues are to be discussed.

There is a ditch on both sides of the road. One ditch avoids transparency in the name of love covering the multitude of sin. The other ditch talks about anything and everything in the name of honesty, full disclosure, and transparency. One must use wisdom to determine the appropriate course of action in the circumstance they are facing. Both of these are correct in the correct application. Your motive is the key in these situations.

Proverbs 27:5 declares, "Open rebuke is better than secret love." That means that it is better for someone to tell another individual the truth than cover it up in the name of love. It is better for an individual to be confronted with the truth than hide the truth from them for the fear of hurting their feelings. Hiding things is not love; it is deception. Love will confront; however, it confronts with the goal of restoration.

Most evil speaking and lying does not happen in this type of arena. It happens within the day-to-day life of believers where things are being said that should not. Things are posted that should not land on the pages of social media.

Venting

Here is a good rule to live by. If you're talking to or about anyone other than a person that can do something about the situation, you're gossiping. Venting is not a reason for malicious negative talking. Venting is a term that attempts to justify words coming out of our mouth that Jesus said would defile us. If you feel you have to vent, then vent to the Lord.

Don't be a confidant for a gossiper. You become just as guilty if you do. If you think you are doing someone a favor by being their ear as they "vent," think again. Allowing someone to sin is not virtuous. Don't enable that type of behavior in others. Stop being their trash can!

If someone begins to speak to you negatively about another individual ask them if they have that individual's phone number so you can call them. They will usually clam up fairly quickly. Jesus said that if you have an issue, then go to them and be reconciled. He didn't say tell everyone in the church. This type of behavior is sinful and breaks the commandment of "you shall not bear false witness."

The heart of the ninth commandment is that we are to speak the truth in love and refrain from speaking evil. This includes false accusations and any other thing that would destroy another individual. I believe by the grace of God we can fulfill this command.

Please pray this prayer with me:

Father God, I make a fresh commitment today to follow Your command to not bear false witness. I appropriate forgiveness for any place within my life where I have broken this command. I receive deliverance and healing as I renounce the hidden works of darkness.

Today, I forsake any and all types of lying and evil speaking. All gossiping, tale-bearing, and backbiting I now re-

nounce. *I choose to speak the truth in love and allow no corrupt communication to come out of my mouth. My tongue will only speak that which is good for the purpose of edifying the church. From this day forward, I will use my tongue as an agent of blessing.*

Thank You for Your grace that empowers and enables me to fulfill Your commandment. Put a watch over my mouth. Thank You, Holy Spirit, for Your ability to live above sin. Sin will not have dominion over me. In the name of Jesus, I pray. Amen.

Notes:

[1] John Wesley, *John Wesley's Notes on the Entire Bible* (Wesley Books, 2010).

[2] Adam Clarke, *Adam Clarke's Commentary on the Bible* (Nashville: Thomas Nelson, Inc, 1997).

CHAPTER TWELVE
THE ETERNAL FOCUS

"You shall not covet your neighbor's house; you shall not covet your neighbor's wife, nor his male servant, nor his female servant, nor his ox, nor his donkey, nor anything that is your neighbor's" (Exodus 20:17).

Here is the last of the Ten Commandments. I believe that it has to be of great importance because it is the last one. There are times that my wife and I will have to go out of town on a trip. When we do, there are things that we emphasize to our staff. It is usually the last thing that we say that it is most important to us. We will even say, "Don't forget this."

Although I am not establishing doctrine with this state-ment, it is very possible that God may have purposefully placed this commandment last for a reason. Perhaps He did this to bring emphasis that we were not to forget this commandment. Covetousness is very dangerous in the life of any person. It can and will destroy someone if it is allowed to operate and func-tion.

Jesus Reinforces the Commandment

Jesus reinforced this commandment. He talked about the danger of covetousness. Let's see what He said.

> And He said to them, "Take heed and beware of covetousness, for one's life does not consist in the abundance of the things he possesses." Then He spoke a parable to them, saying: "The ground of a certain rich man yielded plentifully. And he thought within himself, saying, 'What shall I do, since I have no room to store my crops?' So he said, 'I will do this: I will pull down my barns and build greater, and there I will store all my crops and my goods. And I will say to my soul, "Soul, you have many goods laid up for many years; take your ease; eat, drink, and be merry."' But God said to him, 'Fool! This night your soul will be required of you; then whose will those things be which you have provided?' "So is he who lays up treasure for himself, and is not rich toward God" (Luke 12:15-21).

Jesus begins this passage by saying, "Take heed" and "beware." *Take heed* means to pay attention to this. Jesus was saying that everyone needed to put themselves on guard. It is important not to get snared with the trap of covetousness. It will promise you everything, but only deliver destruction and pain.

Jesus says to "beware." I believe when Jesus says "beware," He means we should stay away from it. There is no secret message in this statement. Jesus says what He means and means what He says. Jesus is saying, "Don't covet." He reinforces the tenth commandment.

It still amazes me how some people say the Ten Commandments are not for us today as believers in the New Testament. It has been evidenced in each chapter of this book how Jesus taught and reinforced all of the Ten Commandments. If He really had wanted to abolish them, He would have clearly articulated it. Jesus was not blinking Morse code to His disciples while saying something contrary.

The Heart of the Commandment

As we read the parable that Jesus gave concerning covetousness, I believe we can see the heart of the commandment. Again, we want to look at each and every commandment through the perspective of grace. I believe the heart of the Father in this commandment is FOCUS ON THE ETERNAL, RATHER THAN THE TEMPORARY.

In the parable of the rich man, we observe a man who has some wonderful traits. He is diligent. He is productive. He is a visionary. However, his downfall is that his eyes are on temporary satisfaction, rather than eternal purpose.

There is no indication that Jesus rebukes the man for his willingness to plant and harvest. That is actually something that God Himself enacted at the beginning of creation. There is nowhere that Jesus indicates the man was evil for building barns. There was no biblical restriction on the size of a man's barn. So, his diligence was not his sin.

The Root of Covetousness

The rich man said, "Soul...take your ease; eat, drink, and be merry." Here we see his sin. Besides the fact that the man had wandered over into a place of trusting his wealth, his main offense was his disposition of accumulation for self-indulgence. He moved to a mental and spiritual disposition of relying on what he had done in previous years to get him through the future ones. The man lost his intensity and began to trust in the fruit of his own labor rather than trust the hand of God to bring blessing continually.

The Greek word that is translated "take your ease" actually means to repose or be exempt. The root word means to stop or quit. Basically, the man quit serving God and started serving himself as he began to pursue the things that he owned. He exempted himself from any future diligence in the area of sowing and reaping because He placed his trust in the things that he possessed.

Jesus is pointing out the fact that covetousness will cause someone to be self-serving and take the wrong course of action. At the root of covetousness is a trust in natural temporary provision. It is the belief that the more provision one has, the more secure their life will be. Covetousness causes one's trust to be misplaced.

Jesus says that a man's life does not consist of the abundance of things that he possesses. The key words are "life" and "things." The life of God is not derived from things. The reality is you can have all the wealth in the world and be miserable. The things that you possess do not define who you are, nor will it determine true happiness and contentment.

You Can't Take It With You

Notice that at the end of the parable the man dies. This man enters eternity, and Jesus asks the question of who's going to own it now. He was saying, 'You can't take it with you.' Jesus is saying in His discourse on covetousness that we must make the eternal our focus. Jesus is cautioning believers to take heed and beware of making the temporary their focus because it leads to covetousness. It leads to accumulation for self-indulging purposes which leads to trusting in wealth and other things. These are things in which God never intended for us to trust.

Jesus points out that we should be rich toward God so that when we pass there will be something on the other side of our earthly existence. This man had nothing. He was not rich toward God. He had spent all of his time focusing on the temporary that is only a fleeting moment in comparison to eternity.

While I believe that God takes pleasure in prospering His people, we should never make accumulation the goal of our lives. While I believe that God makes us the head and not the tail, we should beware of pursuing wealth and riches. We should not use the message of prosperity as an excuse for covetousness. Likewise, we should never use the message of grace as an excuse for willful sin.

The Manifestation of Covetousness

I have found that covetousness manifests primarily in three different ways. It manifests through discontentment and ingratitude. It manifests through envy and jealousy. It also manifests through greed and the love of money. All of these manifestations are sin and works of the flesh.

I want to share some specifics concerning each of these manifestations of breaking the tenth commandment. My desire is to shed some light on some things that are common within the lives of believers. These things will destroy people's lives if they are left unchecked.

Discontentment and ingratitude is one of the first manifestations of covetousness. Most people do not believe they are falling short if they are discontented and ungrateful. However, God has something different to say about that.

> *"Moreover all these curses shall come upon you and pursue and overtake you, until you are destroyed, because you did not obey the voice of the LORD your God, to keep His commandments and His statutes which He commanded you. And they shall be upon you for a sign and a wonder, and on your descendants for-*

ever. Because you did not serve the LORD your God with joy and gladness of heart, for the abundance of everything, therefore you shall serve your enemies, whom the LORD will send against you, in hunger, in thirst, in nakedness, and in need of everything; and He will put a yoke of iron on your neck until He has destroyed you" (Deuteronomy 28:45-48).

The Lord declares here that disobedience to His commands will result in destruction. The New Testament rendition of this would be, "The wages of sin is death" (Romans 6:23). Another way of saying this is: 'Sin has a pay day and you won't like your paycheck.' I know it's been said that sin doesn't pay. In actuality sin does pay. However, its paycheck is unpleasant and will not make you happy.

The Need for Joy, Gladness, and Contentment

In verse forty-seven of the above passage of Scripture, God declares one of the reasons for the curse and destruction. He says, "Because you did not serve the Lord your God with JOY and GLADNESS OF HEART, for the abundance of everything." God says that destruction comes as the result of not being happy and content with the things that you possess.

At the root of covetousness is a discontentment with that which one possesses. At the root of this sin is a belief that if you possessed more or something different you would be happy, content, and joyful. This type of belief is not only misplaced trust, but is also a false dependency. God did not create us to be dependent on things.

Many times people begin to think that they would be happy and content if they were only in a different set of circumstances. My friend, if you can't be happy where you are now, and with whom you're with now, and with what you have now, then a change in your scenario will still fail to make you happy. God did not design us with a contentment dependency based upon those types of things.

I am fully convinced that there is a place in our hearts that only God can fill. When that is filled with Him we will be content. When that is filled with His presence, we will be joyful and happy. The Psalmist said that in the presence of the Lord there is joy, and at His right hand there are pleasures forever-more! Hallelujah!

When covetousness creeps in, it brings an attitude which says, 'If I just had this, I would be good.' Here, we see the deceptiveness of sin. The thinking is: 'This is not a harmful thing; I'm not hurting anyone, and God said I could have it.' The issue here is not the will of God in possessing the things they desire. The real issue is the lack of joy and happiness while those things are not present. The real issue is focusing on the temporary when we should be focusing on the eternal.

Let me qualify some of these statements. There is nothing sinful about wanting something better than what you presently have as long as you remain content with what you have now. For instance, there is nothing wrong with wanting a new car provided you can maintain your joy and gladness without it. If that thing is required for your personal joy, then you are stepping over into covetousness. Dependence is being placed on a temporary item to bring satisfaction into your life. Jesus said that we needed to make the eternal our focus and goal.

The Result of Discontentment

One of the first things that comes to my mind when we talk about discontentment is the children of Israel after they had been delivered from slavery in Egypt. For hundreds of years they had suffered at the hands of the taskmasters in Egypt. They had built cities, monuments, and edifices

throughout the land, yet had no right of ownership or possession. They were slaves in a land that was not their own.

God raises up a deliverer named Moses. He prophesies to
Pharaoh to let God's people be released from captivity and
slavery. Pharaoh hardens his heart to the word of the Lord and
God releases judgment in the way of the plagues. Finally, the
Israelites are released and come out with the wealth of Egypt.
God deals with the Egyptian army at the Red Sea and a mighty
victory is realized.

They eventually reach the Promised Land—the land of
Canaan. Upon arrival, Moses sends in twelve men to spy out the
land. Two of them come back with a good report, and ten of
them come back with a bad report. Unfortunately the ten spies
influence the people and they begin to murmur against Moses
and Aaron.

Let's look at what they said:

> And all the children of Israel complained against Moses
> and Aaron, and the whole congregation said to them,
> "If only we had died in the land of Egypt! Or if only we
> had died in this wilderness! Why has the LORD
> brought us to this land to fall by the sword, that our
> wives and children should become victims? Would it
> not be better for us to return to Egypt?" So they said
> to one another, "Let us select a leader and return to
> Egypt" (Numbers 14:2-4).

After all that God had done to deliver them in the way of
irrefutable signs and wonders, they complained. They murmured. They began to wish for something they did not have.
They longed for something other than what they possessed.
They wanted to be in a different place, among different people,
with a leader other than the one whom God had ordained.

The joy they had upon leaving Egypt had vanished. The elation they experienced as the Egyptians loaded them with their wealth had disappeared. Although they had come out of Egypt, Egypt was still holding them. They were DEPENDENT on something and someone other than the Lord. They were dependent on the government of Pharaoh, the people of Egypt, and the leeks and onions to bring satisfaction to them.

God was not pleased with their response. He tells Moses in Exodus chapter fourteen that He will wipe them out and raise up a nation from just him. Moses intercedes to change the sentence that God pronounced and God responds in mercy by pardoning their offence. Then, God articulates this (understand this is God's mercy and grace that is being extended and then articulated):

> *Then the LORD said: "I have pardoned, according to your word; but truly, as I live, all the earth shall be filled with the glory of the LORD—because all these men who have seen My glory and the signs which I did in Egypt and in the wilderness, and have put Me to the test now these ten times, and have not heeded My voice, they certainly shall not see the land of which I swore to their fathers, nor shall any of those who rejected Me see it."*

> *"How long shall I bear with this evil congregation who complain against Me? I have heard the complaints which the children of Israel make against Me. Say to them, 'As I live,' says the LORD, 'just as you have spoken in My hearing, so I will do to you: The carcasses of you who have complained against Me shall fall in this wilderness, all of you who were numbered, according to your entire number, from twenty years old and above" (Numbers 14:20-23, 27-29).*

An Example from Which to Learn

WOW! This was God's mercy. This was God's grace. This was His forgiveness in manifestation.

We must understand that forgiveness, mercy, and grace do not mean that all consequences of sinful behavior will be eradicated. God pardoned them, but there was still a portion of what God had promised to them that was nullified. This entire account is rearticulated in the New Testament and is given as a warning that we should not fall into the same snare of sin and consequence of disobedience (1 Corinthians 10:10-11).

Their primary offense was murmuring and complaining which was rooted in dissatisfaction and discontentment. They wanted something they did not possess. They were looking for contentment in the wrong place. They were looking for satisfaction from the wrong source. They were coveting something they did not have.

In the above Scripture, God said they tempted Him ten times. How did they tempt Him? They constantly complained and murmured. They were unthankful and unappreciative for that which God had given them. They complained constantly about their circumstances. They complained about their supernatural provision. They murmured about water. They were upset with Moses at the Red Sea immediately after God had delivered them when they were loaded down with the wealth of Egypt. Regardless of what was taking place, they were discontent.

The writer of Hebrews says this is also rooted in unbelief. Understand this, that which God calls unbelief is actually wrong belief. Everyone believes something. It is actually only unbelief when that which you believe is wrong. The Israelites belief was rooted in covetousness. They believed the key to joy, happiness, and contentment was increase, wealth, and agreeable circumstances. They probably picked this up from the Egyptians. However, what they believed was contrary to God's word and promise. Therefore, it was unbelief.

Envy—Despising One for Their Possessions

The next manifestation of covetousness is envy and jealousy. We must understand that the commandment to not covet indicates that we are to live free from envy and jealousy. Let's start by focusing on envy.

Envy is the despising of another person because of that which they possess. It is the love reduction for someone who has more than another. The more they possess, the less love one has for them. The fact that an individual has certain possessions agitates and irritates the one who is envious. This is what is at the root of "class warfare" (about which we will talk later).

That which people despise others for having is usually what they wish they possessed themselves. It is that which they are coveting. They become angry in the fact that someone they know has something that they want themselves. It causes one to despise others solely for that which they have in their possession.

Here is an important principle for you to understand. Anything you despise another for having will never be released into your life. Why would God release anything in your life that you despise someone else for having? Think about it.

Envy repels the blessing of God in your life. You end up living resentful and bitter because of the things that others have which you do not possess. This is a miserable existence.

The Bible says that envy and jealousy are cruel as the grave (Song of Solomon 8:6). It will cause you to feel like you are continually dying. It will rob you of joy and happiness. It will steal the life from you. My friend, it's not worth it. Let go of envy.

Celebration Brings Attraction

Understand this: whatever you celebrate, you will attract. When you see someone else blessed, rejoice with them. If you see someone else receive a new car, start rejoicing with them rather than be bitter about it. You may have believed God for a longer period of time. You may even think you're more dedicated to the Lord. However, despising God's blessing on the life of another is envy that is born out of covetousness.

Understand that envy and jealousy act as agents that repel that which one desires. It is a vicious circle. Someone begins to covet and long for something which in turn produces envy and jealousy. Their envy and jealousy repels what they are coveting. The end result is they live with unfulfilled desire all their days unless they result to thievery. This is not God's plan for any of us.

The exact opposite is also true. When someone sees another experiencing blessing and increase, they begin to celebrate and be joyous. The force of joy released within their life attracts what they are celebrating in the lives of others. God said that the lack of joy and gladness of heart for the abundance of all things (regardless of whose life it is manifested) would cause the curse to be manifested. However, the existence of joy and gladness of heart for the abundance of all things will cause the blessing of the Lord to be manifested. If covetousness brings the curse, then contentment and joy will receive the blessing. I trust you are seeing this principle.

Class Warfare

I mentioned earlier about the danger of what we have termed as "class warfare." Class warfare is that which pits those who have little money and possessions against those who have much. It divides people based on socio-economic status. It is a destructive force that has its roots in the sin of coveting.

Anytime that anyone is bitter toward someone else because of their perceived wealth, success, or possessions, it is envy and jealousy which is covetousness. It is sin, and it is wrong. There is no justification for it. Class warfare is sin. Believing that someone who has wealth owes a portion of it to those who are not as fortunate is covetousness and sin. If I have less than someone else and I believe that they owe me part of what they have solely because they have more than me, then I am operating in covetousness. My friend, no matter how you slice it, it is sin!

Class warfare is rooted in covetousness because it is nothing more than envy and jealousy renamed. It is wrong. It is ungodly. We should avoid it and those who promote it. Anyone who promotes others to sin should be avoided. Witness to them, but avoid them. Paul said that evil communications corrupts good manners. Don't get corrupted by those who practice ignorance and sin.

The Love of Money

The last manifestation of covetousness is the love of money. It is conduct that makes money the goal of one's life. It is the place where people compromise their once held convictions for the purpose of the dollar. Paul talked about the love of money and the dangers of it.

"For the love of money is the root of all evil: which while some coveted after, they have erred from the faith, and pierced themselves through with many sorrows" (1 Timothy 6:10, KJV).

Notice what Paul says. Those who have COVETED money have erred from the faith and pierced themselves with sorrow. This is not good. Erring from the faith is not good. Piercing yourself with sorrow is not good.

Let me say it like this: loving money is self-destructive. You destroy yourself when you love money. The devil doesn't have to do anything. Covetousness causes people to hurt themselves. It is shooting one's self in the foot. How crazy is that?

Understand that loving money has absolutely nothing to do with how much money you possess. You can love money and not have a dime to your name. Loving money is an attitude and disposition toward money. It is the approach that one takes towards wealth.

Jesus talked about the dangers of loving money. He said that you cannot serve God and money (Matthew 6:24). He declared that those who love money would not be able to enter into the kingdom of God. Why would they not be able to enter into the kingdom of God? It's because loving money is the sin of coveting.

Jesus explained to His disciples that loving money is actually trusting in money. Money was never supposed to be loved; it is designed to be used as an exchange for goods that are needed. It is for the use of purchasing things we need in the natural world where we live.

Money itself is not bad. It is the love of money that is sin. I've seen those who have abundance and do not love money. I've witnessed others who had nearly nothing and loved money. So the love of money is not determined by how much you possess. It is determined by your disposition toward it.

Unfortunately, many in the church today love money. They have also falsely justified it by the misuse of Scripture. The promises of God concerning financial increase and prosperity do not give us an excuse for loving money and coveting.

God gave His promise so we can believe and then see Him provide what we need. The promise was never given to justify what He has already labeled as sinful. It is bad enough to love money, but to use the Bible as a justification is twice the sin.

The Pursuit of Money

I have seen Christians pursue money. They ultimately lose their family, ministry, and relationships with others. Paul said the love of money culminates with sorrow and destruction. I have witnessed it transpire more times than I care to talk about. As a pastor, it breaks my heart to see believers go down that road. However, even when many are warned, they persist.

The pursuit of money and covetousness will spiritually blind someone. They get to a point where all they live for is the temporary. Their lives are consumed with that which is passing. All of their effort and time is invested in the accumulation of wealth. Ultimately they self-destruct.

Most every pastor I know can give accounts of these types of things happening to people within their congregation. They come to the church for the first time in despair. Their lives are then transformed by the Word of God and the ministry of the Holy Spirit. They are faithful to the house of the Lord and faithful to give their tithes and offerings, and God blesses them abundantly.

The next thing that happens is the new found blessing becomes a snare. They purchase a boat, a RV, a condo at the beach, and anything else they can afford. Now, the thing that once ministered life to them (the Word of God, the Holy Spirit, the church, etc.) is interfering with their enjoyment of life and family time. They stop attending church regularly because they must enjoy all the blessings that God has lavished on them. They stop tithing and giving offerings because now they need some of that money to service the debt they have created.

The story continues. They finally get to the place where they no longer attend church or serve God. They backslide and their family falls to pieces. They lose all that God originally restored to them and sometimes more. Why? It's because they pursued the temporary rather than focusing on the eternal.

Fool!

In the parable of the rich man that we read at the beginning of this chapter, Jesus said that the rich man said to himself, "Take your ease; eat, drink, and be merry." It's interesting to see the response of God. He calls the man, "Fool!" The only time we ever specifically read about God calling someone a fool is in a parable where Jesus is talking about covetousness. Could it be that the practice of covetous behavior makes one a fool? According to Jesus it does. Think about it.

Jesus said that a man's life does not consist of the abundance of things he possesses. Things do not define you. Wealth does not define you. Those things are here for us to enjoy but not be the focus of our lives. We must understand that coveting happens when one gets their focus off the eternal. It is the eternal that is most important. At the end of the day, it is the eternal that will define you.

In the modern culture we live in today it is easy to be distracted from eternal things. We have television, internet, social media, and many other things that are constantly bidding for our focus and attention. Advertisements tell us what we must have to be considered successful, how we must look to be accepted, and who we need to be like to be esteemed. They will tell the viewer, "To be somebody you must own this." The goal of these advertisements is to motivate the observer to spend money. If one doesn't have money or the thing they need to be considered successful then they will begin to long for it. This longing for the temporary as it escalates can become covetousness and destroy one's life.

Focusing on the Eternal

I know you are probably asking, "How do I focus on the eternal?" Understand that focusing on the eternal is not living in a manner where you think only about heaven. It is not living so spiritually minded that you are of no earthly good. It is not living in a super-spiritual state where you cannot function here on earth.

Here are some practical things to practice in order to focus on the eternal and prevent covetousness.

The Thankful Heart

First of all, live with a thankful heart. I'm referring to a heart that is turned toward the Father God in appreciation for every way you have been blessed. Thanksgiving is an important part of the life of any believer. We are to offer up the sacrifice of praise which is the "fruit of our lips giving thanks unto His name" (Hebrews 13:15).

Thanksgiving will prevent murmuring and complaining. Thanksgiving will fortify you against covetous behavior. Being thankful for what you have will prevent you from longing with intense desire for something that you don't have. Thanksgiving will keep you from being tormented.

A Family Focus

The second thing is live with a family focus. I have told the members in our church that I consider myself the richest man on earth. I have a wonderful wife who loves the Lord, loves me, and loves our children. We have three wonderful children who love God, love their parents, and are serving the Lord. We have four grandchildren that are all healthy and growing. Everyone in our family is healthy. None of us have missed a meal.

I could live on the side of the street in a cardboard box and still consider myself rich! The fact that all my family is serving God makes me a wealthy man. These are eternal things. These are things that will still be around after the cars have hit the scrapheap. These are things that will have lasting value long after the house and 401K have depreciated because of temporary economic conditions. A family focus helps to put everything in proper perspective.

A Spirit of Generosity

The third thing is live with a spirit of generosity. Live to give rather than live to accumulate. Giving is a weapon of spiritual warfare against the spirit of greed and covetousness. When someone cannot give, it means they are trusting in that which they cannot release. It means their faith is in the money which they cannot turn loose.

God promises blessing to those who give. He said that our barns would be filled with plenty and our vats would overflow with new wine and oil as we honor Him with the first-fruits of all of our increase (Proverbs 3:10). That means that as we are faithful with our tithe (the first ten percent of our income), God will pour out abundantly within our lives. Paul said that God loves a cheerful giver. He went on to say that God would cause the cheerful giver to have more than enough of all things. I don't have to pursue things because they will come on me supernaturally as I practice generosity.

Trust God

The last thing is to live trusting God. The Bible says, "Cursed is the man who trusts in man and makes flesh his strength, whose heart departs from the Lord" (Jeremiah 17:5). Someone who is trusting in their own labor will not rely on God, because their heart has departed from Him. They work frantically to ensure they have enough because they are relying on their own ability. Think about the bizarreness of this condition: to trust man's ability over the strength of God who created all of heaven and earth.

We should trust Him and not our own labor and work. Remember that one moment of God's favor is worth a lifetime of your labor. We should trust in the favor of God rather than what we can produce through putting our nose to the grindstone. That gives no one an excuse for laziness and idleness. However, trusting the arm of the flesh produces the curse. The Psalmist said, "I have not seen the righteous forsaken nor his seed begging bread" (Psalm 37:25). God will take care of those who trust Him. I'm going to trust Him.

Make a choice today to focus on the eternal. It will keep you from covetousness. It will bring the blessing of the Lord. It will open the door for God to bless you beyond your dreams. You won't have to chase blessings. Blessings will chase you and tackle you! Hallelujah!

Please pray this prayer with me:

Father God, I make a fresh commitment today to follow Your command to not covet. I appropriate forgiveness for any place within my life where I have broken this command. I receive deliverance and healing as I renounce the hidden works of darkness.

Today, I forsake any and all types of covetousness. I choose to make eternal things the focus of my life. I make a fresh heart commitment to pursue You and trust You. Thank You for bringing blessing and provision within my life. Thank You for Your grace that empowers and enables me to fulfill Your commandment. Thank You for power and ability to live above sin. Sin will not have dominion over me. In Jesus' name. Amen.

CHAPTER THIRTEEN

THE SPIRIT OF LAWLESSNESS

"Not everyone who says to Me, 'Lord, Lord,'
shall enter the kingdom of heaven, but he
who does the will of My Father in heaven.
Many will say to Me in that day, 'Lord, Lord,
have we not prophesied in Your name, cast
out demons in Your name, and done many
wonders in Your name?' And then I will de-
clare to them, 'I never knew you; depart from
Me, you who practice lawlessness!'"
(Matthew 7:21-23)

I would like to share some things in this chapter dealing with the spirit of lawlessness. This is something that has crept into the church at large. There has been an accelerated amount of it over the last several decades.

Simply put, the spirit of lawlessness is that which causes Christians to live without law—to live void of the righteous moral standard that God dictated. It is that which excuses sinful behavior and will at times encourage it in an attempt to prove the existence of freedom. It is dangerous and needs to be identified and removed from the lives of believers.

Jesus identified it in this passage of Scripture. He speaks specifically of the end result of those who practice lawlessness. He says, "Depart from me." It can be debated exactly what is meant when Jesus said this; yet, I believe we can all agree that we don't want to hear those words. It can be argued as to where the people who heard these words actually departed. However, I certainly do not want to be a part of that crowd.

Balance and the Full Counsel

These verses of Scripture bring balance to teaching on mercy and grace. Jesus' teaching here is in no way contrary to grace. It actually brings to light the whole counsel of God. Understand that anytime someone takes a Scripture or Scriptures and creates a doctrine from it while ignoring other verses, it will become error. Error always lives right next door to truth. Error is not located a thousand miles away from that which is correct. It's just a few houses down the road.

There are Scriptures that we all have knowledge of that would almost seem contradictory to that which Jesus said. For instance, the verse which says, "I will never leave you or forsake you," seems somewhat opposing. However, it is not. The Scriptures together help paint a picture of the full counsel of God—the full gospel.

There is a real need in the church today to hear the full counsel of God. Hearing only about the blessing of the Lord without hearing the resulting consequences of disobedience will cause believers to be warped—warped in their thinking and believing. They become lopsided in their understanding of the Father God.

Their understanding of the Father becomes like that of Santa Claus—just without the naughty list. God becomes someone who is pouring out gifts and toys regardless to how they live their lives. There is never a word of correction that comes from Him. There is never a consequence for unrighteous behavior.

Eventually, when sin's payday arrives, they get mad and bitter at God. They feel that God has failed them. They leave the church like a pouting child because God did not perform what they had been told He would do regardless of their manner of living. They had never heard there would be a consequence for disobedience and now they feel that they were told a lie. The reality is that the seed of sin that they sowed through lawless behavior brought forth a harvest.

To Whom Did Jesus Say "Depart"?

Looking back at the passage of Scripture that started this chapter, we can see some characteristics of the ones that Jesus said to "depart." The **first** thing He said is that they confessed Him as Lord. They said to Jesus, "Lord, Lord." It could be reasoned that these people had made a decision for Jesus. It could be assumed that they had been led in a sinner's prayer.

The **second** thing we see about these people is that they preached and prophesied. They knew how to hear the voice of the Holy Spirit. It could even be said that they had some knowledge of the Word of God. Since we prophesy according to the proportion of our faith, they had revelation of God's Word and the Holy Spirit. It appears they had understanding of the power of the name of Jesus since they were doing all of these things in His name.

The **third** thing we see about these people is that they practiced deliverance. They cast out demonic spirits. They knew their authority. They possessed an anointing to liberate those who were bound by the devil.

The **fourth** thing we see about these people is that they were having miracles in their ministry. There were healings and miraculous manifestations of the Holy Spirit. There were things happening within their ministry that were causing people to be astonished at the display of the power of God. They were being invited everywhere because people were desirous to receive of the anointing that rested upon them.

All of these things sound wonderful. As a matter of fact, these are things ministers and believers have been commissioned to do. Jesus said in Mark chapter sixteen that "these signs will follow them that believe." He goes on to speak of the very things that they were doing. So none of these things mentioned are the reason that Jesus would say for them to depart.

However, there is one more characteristic that Jesus mentions that many fail to see. That is this: they practiced lawlessness. It was their practice of lawlessness that prompted Jesus to say, "Depart from me." It was not their performance of ministry that was their downfall. It was the lack of performance of moral law. They were lawless.

Understand that supernatural manifestations within someone's ministry are not God's stamp of approval on their lifestyle. The people Jesus talks about here are those who are seeing mighty displays of God's power and anointing. However, they possess a lawless lifestyle. They are not those who fall, are convicted, repent, and then move forward. These are those who sin to a point of having a seared conscious.

What It Means to Be Lawless

The Greek word used here for "lawlessness" is **anomia**. It means illegality and violation of law. Lawlessness is living in violation of law. It is living without or ignoring the law; it is the breaking of law.

Now get this: you cannot violate something that does not exist. The only way someone can be lawless is for there to be law in existence that is being broken. So then the question arises of what law is Jesus talking about that they are breaking? I'm glad you asked.

Jesus answers that question in the verses immediately following:

"Therefore whoever hears these sayings of Mine, and does them, I will liken him to a wise man who built his house on the rock: and the rain descended, the floods came, and the winds blew and beat on that house; and it did not fall, for it was founded on the rock. But everyone who hears these sayings of Mine, and does not do them, will be like a foolish man who built his house on the sand: and the rain descended, the floods came, and the winds blew and beat on that house; and it fell. And great was its fall." (Matthew 7:24-27).

The lawlessness that Jesus was referring to was the failure to obey what He said. In verse twenty-six, He refers to those who hear His sayings and do not obey them. The ones who practice lawlessness are those who disobey the words of Jesus.

Throughout this book we have repeatedly revealed some of the words of Jesus. He said, "Don't commit adultery," "Don't lie," "Don't murder," and many other things contained within the Ten Commandments. Do you think those might be considered the sayings of Jesus since He said it? Or do you think that Jesus spoke about the Ten Commandments, but we are exempt from those words? My friend, Jesus did not say something for us to hear and then exempt us from follow through and obedience. His expectation is compliance to what He said.

The Plague of Lawlessness

Lawlessness is a plague in the church today that needs to be eradicated. Unfortunately, many excuse the practice of lawlessness in the name of freedom from law. They say, "We are not under the law." However, they fail to acknowledge that Paul commanded that believers were not to use freedom as an excuse to walk in the works of the flesh and sin (Galatians 5:13).

It is true that we are not under priestly and ceremonial law as Jesus fulfilled all of it. However, moral law that is contained in the Ten Commandments, which Jesus rearticulated and taught, is still in effect. It still has relevance to those in the

New Covenant. The practice of disobeying these commandments is the practice of lawlessness.

In response to those who say we are not under law, I want to examine a Scripture:

> If you really fulfill the royal law according to the Scripture, "YOU SHALL LOVE YOUR NEIGHBOR AS YOURSELF," you do well; but if you show partiality, you commit sin, and are convicted by the law as transgressors. For whoever shall keep the whole law, and yet stumble in one point, he is guilty of all. For He who said, "DO NOT COMMIT ADULTERY," also said, "DO NOT MURDER." Now if you do not commit adultery, but you do murder, you have become a transgressor of the law. So speak and so do as those who will be judged by the law of liberty (James 2:8-12).

I want to point out several things. **First** of all, you cannot fulfill a law that does not exist. If there is no law to be fulfilled, then why did James talk about fulfilling the royal law? The obvious conclusion is there is a law to be fulfilled which is love your neighbor as yourself. We've already spoken some about this in a previous chapter.

The **second** thing I want to call your attention to is James articulates some of the Ten Commandments. He didn't say they are not relevant. He didn't say they had passed away. He didn't say you should disregard anything concerning them. He actually reinforces them.

The **third** thing I want you to observe is that as he speaks to believers, he says that one who breaks one of the Ten Commandments becomes a transgressor of the law. The question I have is how can you transgress a law unless it exists and is applicable? Again, the obvious answer is there is law that exists in the New Testament. James emphasizes that the moral law contained in the Ten Commandments still exists.

The Law of Liberty

The last thing I want to point out is the term "law of liberty." Understand this: we are free in Jesus, but that freedom has law and parameters. Those of us who are citizens of the United States of America live in a free nation, yet at the same time there are laws. The majority of those laws are good. They help to maintain order, civility, and life. Can you imagine a nation with no laws? What would that look like? I would not want to live there.

It's interesting to me that James mentions the law of liberty in connection with the Ten Commandments. Immediately following the mention of two of these commandments he says "so speak and so do." He was actually saying we should be doers of the Word.

This goes back to the parable that Jesus gave of the man who built his house upon the rock. The foolish man was the one who heard the Word, yet disobeyed. The wise man was the one who heard and obeyed.

Look at what James says about the law of liberty:

"But he who looks into the perfect law of liberty and continues in it, and is not a forgetful hearer but a doer of the work, this one will be blessed in what he does" (James 1:25).

This is in perfect harmony with what Jesus said after His discourse concerning those who practice lawlessness. He said the ones who practice lawlessness are those who hear and then forget and disobey. James referred to those who look into the law of liberty and continue in it. He was talking about those who hear and obey. Jesus spoke of that person as a wise man.

Although, notice that James said this in relationship to the law of liberty. Understand that the law of liberty is not living without law. The law of liberty is living a lifestyle of obedience and adherence to moral law that will keep you liberated. It is the law of liberty that keeps you from bondage and the consequence of sin. You choose to obey commandments that prevent you from entering back into the bondage of sin.

Living free from law is not freedom. My friend, that leads to bondage. A manner of life that ignores the moral directives and commands that Jesus dictated will surely end up in disaster. Jesus said that it would. No person that lives without law will come out on the other side blessed of the Lord. James said the person continuing in the LAW of liberty would be blessed.

The Destiny of the Lawless

"The Son of Man will send out His angels, and they will gather out of His kingdom all things that offend, and those who practice lawlessness, and will cast them into the furnace of fire. There will be wailing and gnashing of teeth" (Matthew 13:41-42).

Here once again, Jesus talks about those who practice lawlessness. We could also refer to them as those who live with no law. Jesus declares that He will gather out of His kingdom those who practice lawlessness and cast them into the furnace of fire (don't expect to hear that preached in most of our post-modern churches). While it could be argued as to what the furnace of fire may be, I believe we will all agree that this is not the place to be. No one wants to be a part of the group that is cast into the furnace of fire.

But Jesus says that this is the destiny of those who practice lawlessness. He says that this is where that road leads. The road of lawlessness is like driving out into an endless dessert with no water. You will end up dry and dying. It will bring catastrophe and calamity. Friend, it's not worth it.

The Ten Commandments and Bondage

Tell me, you who desire to be under the law, do you not hear the law? or it is written that Abraham had two sons: the one by a bondwoman, the other by a freewoman. But he who was of the bondwoman was born according to the flesh, and he of the freewoman through promise, which things are symbolic. For these are the two covenants: the one from Mount Sinai which gives birth to bondage, which is Hagar— for this Hagar is Mount Sinai in Arabia, and corresponds to Jerusalem which now is, and is in bondage with her children—but the Jerusalem above is free, which is the mother of us all (Galatians 4:21-26).

There are some that have used this passage of Scripture to assert that the Ten Commandments are bondage. The argument is that since these commandments were given at Mount Sinai, they give birth to bondage. They go on to say that the Ten Commandments are Old Covenant law and no longer applicable to us. However, that is not what this Scripture says.

The **first** thing to address is to whom Paul is speaking. He is speaking to believers who wanted to go back under ceremonial law. These were Gentiles who were deceived into putting themselves under Levitical law after they were saved. This involved things (such as circumcision) which were unnecessary for salvation or holy living (Galatians 5:6). Jesus fulfilled and abolished all of these things in his substitutionary act on the cross.

There is no need for a blood sacrifice because Jesus became the sacrifice once and for all. There is no need for celebrations of feasts because it is unnecessary to embrace the shadow of things to come when you have the real thing. There is no need for circumcision since there is a spiritual circumcision that takes place at the time of the new birth. The things required in the ceremonial law that pointed to Jesus are no longer necessary since Jesus accomplished all of it.

Secondly, we see in verse twenty-four that Paul says these things are symbolic. He goes on to say that Mount Sinai corresponds to Jerusalem in its present condition. What was their present condition? They had rejected Jesus. This primarily was stated in reference to Jerusalem's rejection of Jesus as the Messiah. It was not in reference to the Ten Commandments since many were already rearticulated by Paul.

To say that in this passage of Scripture, Paul was implying that the Ten Commandments are meaningless is to accuse Paul of being double-minded. He quotes many of these commandments throughout his writings. I believe Paul was an intelligent man and not confused when he quoted them. Just the fact that he quotes the commandment of honoring your father and mother to the Ephesians solidifies the fact that the Commandments are still applicable to us who are part of the New Covenant.

This is the reality: we cannot live lawlessly (void of law). It is sinful. It produces bad fruit. In the previous passage of Scripture, Jesus talked about lawlessness. He also talked about knowing a tree by the fruit it bears (Matthew 12:33). If someone is producing the fruit of sin, then it is a lawless tree. If the lifestyle of a believer is filled with sinful activity with no conviction, then they are a lawless tree. By their fruit you will know them.

The Need for Revival, Repentance, and Righteousness

There is much more that I could write on the subject of lawlessness. It is an epidemic in the church today. We all need to pray that repentance would come to the body of Christ. We should pray for a revival that returns conviction and righteous living. We need to return to the law of God that is written upon our hearts. We need to return to the Ten Commandments. What a great starting place. The things that God says are always a good place to start. God's law that was restated in the New Testament is a wonderful place to begin.

My friend, as we do this God will bless us in abundance. He will pour out His Spirit in an unprecedented manner. We will see great and mighty things as we choose to follow and obey the Ten Commandments. Remember, grace raised the bar. The heart of God in the commandments was to provide a road map for experiencing life.

God's Law and Blessing

Blessed is the man Who walks not in the counsel of the ungodly, Nor stands in the path of sinners, Nor sits in the seat of the scornful; But his delight is in the law of the LORD, And in His law he meditates day and night. He shall be like a tree Planted by the rivers of water, That brings forth its fruit in its season, Whose leaf also shall not wither; And whatever he does shall prosper (Psalm 1:1-3).

The Psalmist David had an understanding that is needed in the church today. He said that meditating on God's law would cause one to be fruitful and prosper. He said that one would be blessed. That doesn't sound like bondage to me; that sounds like blessing. Bondage comes as the result of law rejection which is lawlessness. Blessing comes as the result of law reception which is obedience.

What do you want? Living in a lawless manner will produce the curse. Living in an obedient manner will produce life. God told His people that He placed before them blessing and cursing, death and life. He then exhorted them to choose life by obeying His commandments. I'm choosing life. What about you?

CHAPTER FOURTEEN
THE LAW OF LOVE

*"But take careful heed to do the commandment
and the law which Moses the servant of the
LORD commanded you, to love the LORD your
God, to walk in all His ways, to keep His com-
mandments, to hold fast to Him, and to serve
Him with all your heart and with all your soul."
(Joshua 22:5)*

In this passage of Scripture, Joshua refers to loving the Lord as law. Notice that he says, "Take careful heed to do the command-ment and the LAW...to LOVE the LORD your God..." LOVE is not a feeling but rather a LAW that is to be acted upon. You don't feel LAW, you obey it. LOVE is never determined by emotions but rather acts of obedience.

We must understand that LOVE is a verb. It is something that you do, rather than something that you feel. However, doing the actions of love will result in corresponding feelings. Doing the right thing will ultimately produce the right emotions.

Love Is Not Emotionally Based

There are many today who believe that love is something that it isn't. Their view of love is that it is present when there are coinciding feelings of appreciation and attraction, but is not existent when these emotions are missing. Their perspective of love is based solely upon what is produced within the mind, emotions, and flesh of human beings. Their view is not based on that which man can choose to do regardless of his feelings.

Any law should be followed whether one feels like obeying it or not. It should never be up for debate based upon the feeling that is present at that moment. A law should be obeyed at all times. A law should be observed even in the face of opposing feelings.

Someone who feels that they should speed one hundred miles an hour on the highway is not justified in breaking the speed limit because of their feelings. Flashing blue lights will quickly show up behind them regardless of their feelings, and they will be given a citation that will definitely make them feel lousy. The conclusion of all of this is that we cannot live by our feelings. We must live by laws that govern our behavior.

Therefore, to truly walk in LOVE, there must be an understanding that it is a LAW that should be obeyed at all times. It is a command that must be followed in order to see and experience the blessings of the Lord. Let's look at what Jesus had to say about the relationship between LAW and LOVE.

Love Keeps the Commandments

"If you love Me, keep My commandments" (John 14:15).

Jesus says that love is acted out in the keeping of His commandments. Since Jesus taught on the Ten Commandments and rearticulated them all, do you think that they may be the commandments He was talking about? I believe so. Therefore, walking in love will cause one to obey the law. It will cause one to obey the commandments that Jesus taught us. The reason for this is that LOVE itself is a LAW. James referred to LOVE as the royal LAW (James 2:8).

One of the reasons that I continue articulating the word LAW throughout this book is because it has been a misunderstood word by many Christians. It is a word that has been vilified by many within the church. We must understand that LAW is a good word and is designed to maintain life and peace. If you don't believe that, go to a country where anarchy and lawlessness are the rule.

Again, LOVE is a LAW. It is commanded in both the Old Testament and the New Testament. The understanding of LOVE is expounded and explained to a greater degree by Jesus, Paul, James, and John in the New Testament. It is revealed that when one walks in LOVE, he will fulfill the LAW. Why? It's because LOVE is a LAW that fulfills the LAW. The actions of one who is obeying the LAW of LOVE will result in every other LAW being fulfilled.

The Power to Love

Here is where it gets interesting. The reality of life places us in contact with unlovely people. There are people who are absolutely impossible to love in your own power and strength. So, where do we derive the strength and power to walk in love when surrounded by the unlovely?

To find the answer to this question we must go to the Bible. Let's see what the Apostle Paul had to say.

"Now hope does not disappoint, because the love of God has been poured out in our hearts by the Holy Spirit who was given to us" (Romans 5:5).

Paul says that the love of God is in our hearts. Therefore, the ability to love is already present; it is on the inside of us. This is the reason we must be born again. The love of God is only available through the new birth. We don't have the capacity to love the unlovely without the nature of God which can only be received through the new birth.

So, when we are born again, our spirit man is recreated and His love is imparted into our lives. This LOVE is a LAW that works inside of us that motivates us to fulfill the commandments that are at the same time written upon our hearts.

This is what is so wonderful: at the same moment that LAW is written on your heart, LOVE is imparted to your spirit man. It is that LAW of LOVE that empowers you to fulfill the LAW that is written upon your heart by the Holy Spirit. Hallelujah!

Love and Law

The LAW of LOVE says that I will do what is right even when I feel like doing something wrong. The LAW of LOVE says that I do unto others as I would want others to do to me. The LAW of LOVE says that as I sow love, I will reap a harvest of love. The LAW of LOVE says that I am enabled to obey God's commandments through the activation of His love within my life.

> Owe no one anything except to love one another, for he who loves another has fulfilled the law. For the command-ments, "YOU SHALL NOT COMMIT ADULTERY," "YOU SHALL NOT MURDER," "YOU SHALL NOT STEAL," "YOU SHALL NOT BEAR FALSE WITNESS," "YOU SHALL NOT COVET," and if there is any other command-ment, are all summed up in this saying, namely, "YOU SHALL LOVE YOUR NEIGHBOR AS YOURSELF." Love does no harm to a neighbor; therefore love is the fulfill-ment of the law (Romans 13:8-10).

Paul declares that LOVE is the fulfillment of the LAW. We understand that no law can be fulfilled outside of obedience and ad-herence to it. So, Paul is saying that as we allow the LAW of LOVE to operate within our lives, we will obey and adhere to the LAW. We will fulfill the commandments that were once written on tablets of stone and are now written on our hearts.

The Appealing Message

There are many topics and messages that are contained in the gospel that Jesus preached. Each topic and message appeals to different people for differing reasons. Unfortunately, some of these appeal to different individuals for the wrong reason.

Let me give you an example. The message of financial blessing and prosperity is a biblical message that needs to be proclaimed. However, it can be especially appealing for the wrong reason to those who practice covetousness. They see the message as a justification for their transgression. They declare that they are merely going after the blessing of the Lord. It is sinful to practice covetousness, but to use the Word as its justification is twice the offense. This is the reason it is imperative that the balance of the Word be preached and proclaimed. The part that we call the balance is usually the part that confronts sin and deals with personal responsibility.

The message of grace and love is a wonderful message and one that needs to be proclaimed uncompromisingly. However, it appeals to some for the wrong reason, particularly to those who are uncommitted and living a life of sin and rebellion. It appeals to them because they hear it incorrectly. To them a message of grace gives them an excuse to behave however they so desire.

The Cry for Balance

Once again, this is the reason that balance must be proclaimed and promoted from the pulpits. Grace and love do not excuse sinful behavior. **Grace and love cause our responsibility to be greater since we are now empowered by the Holy Spirit.** Unfortunately, this is not what most Christians hear because only one side of the message is primarily preached.

Paul said, "Consider the goodness and severity of God" (Romans 11:22). When is the last time you heard the "severity of God" mentioned? I would guess that over 90% of believers today have never heard it at all. However, I can almost guarantee that all Christians have repeatedly heard about the goodness of God. It is not that we should cease to hear about God's goodness, it's just that we need to hear the other equally to be balanced.

The same can be said for the topic and message of LOVE. We need to not only hear about God's LOVE for us, but also the responsibilities that have been delegated to us in the way of loving God and loving people (which is the fulfilling of the Ten Commandments). Everyone wants to be loved. Most do not have an issue with receiving God's LOVE for them; however, fewer are willing to put LOVE into practice. We must comprehend both sides of the equation.

Love Is Proactive

Understand that LOVE is not passive. LOVE is powerful. LOVE takes an aggressive stand against that which is evil. LOVE is what will compel you to fight for your family. LOVE is that which will cause you to get out of bed in the morning and pray for God's intervention in the lives of those who are on the path of destruction. LOVE is proactive!

LOVE takes a stand against sin because they contradict each other. LOVE motivates you to walk in righteousness because that is its nature. LOVE is revealed in what you do rather than how you feel at a given moment. LOVE is revealed through righteous living and holiness.

Love Revealed through Obedience

When Jesus talked about LOVE, it was always connected to action rather than emotion.

"Greater love has no one than this, than to lay down one's life for his friends" (John 15:13).

Laying down one's life is an action as opposed to a feeling. Jesus did not FEEL like laying down His life for anybody. In the Garden of Gethsemane, He wrestled in prayer until His sweat became as great drops of blood. He did not FEEL like going to the cross. He did not FEEL like being beaten and bruised. His action was not based on His FEELINGS. However, He willingly subjected Himself to it all because of His LOVE for us. His LOVE was demonstrated in what He did in spite of how He felt.

God's LOVE manifested will always induce acts of obedience. Jesus said, "Not My will, but Yours, be done" (Luke 22:42). LOVE was revealed through submission to the will of the Father; not a feeling of great anticipation and joy concerning going to the cross. The writer of Hebrews declares that for the joy set before Him, Jesus endured the cross. Enduring something does not mean that you look forward to it.

Disobedience Is the Absence Of Love

It is important for us to understand that disobedience to LAW reveals the absence of LOVE in demonstration. Why? It is because LOVE will always manifest in the conformity and obedience to moral LAW. LOVE will always result in obedience to God's commandments and directives.

For instance, I cannot truthfully say I LOVE someone because of a fond feeling that I possess towards them and at the same time steal from them. It is impossible to LOVE and steal at the same time. Loving and stealing are antithetical to each other. I realize that most people already realize this basic principle. However, the ones that I have personally heard talk the loudest about grace and love in an attempt to avert righteous living are the ones who walk in love the least.

Love Demands

We must understand that LOVE requires something of us. True LOVE demands to be fulfilled. LOVE is not void of works. LOVE will produce good works and righteous living.

It is LOVE in action that keeps marriages together. It is not continual fond feelings that keep husbands and wives married. The reality is that all marriages go through times and seasons where they are challenged. There are disagreements and conflicts that have to be resolved. During these times, the fond feelings toward each other can diminish. These are just the facts of real living that happen in all marital relationships.

So, how do husbands and wives stay in covenant and maintain their commitments during times of challenge and adversity? My friend, it is the fact that they CHOOSE to LOVE in spite of how they feel at that given moment. LOVE will keep its covenant. LOVE will maintain its commitment. LOVE moves beyond the realm of emotion into the realm of obedience to moral LAW and the thing that is right.

It is LOVE that keeps husbands and wives faithful to one another. It is LOVE that keeps them from having an adulterous relationship, not just a healthy sexual relationship between the two of them. It is LOVE that compels them to reconcile following a disagreement. It is LOVE that rids the relationship of selfishness and narcissistic behavior. LOVE causes consideration of the other party to become paramount.

Correct Understanding

There have been many books that have been written on love. There have been teaching series that have been produced along with music and songs that are too many to talk about. In the last two decades in the church, we have probably heard more about love than any other time on record. However, Christians, in general, are more lawless than ever.

I believe it is because of the misunderstanding of LOVE that has disconnected it from LAW. LOVE and LAW are not antagonistic. If they were, LOVE could not fulfill the LAW. LOVE and LAW are inseparable because LOVE is a LAW in itself.

I encourage you today to receive this understanding. It will make a difference in your life. You will no longer live by your emotions that may fluctuate and change. You will live by the LAW of LOVE that provokes righteous living and conformity to that which God has declared and required. Make this declaration with me:

> "Today I choose to LOVE. In doing so, I fulfill the LAW. I fulfill and obey the Ten Commandments as I walk in love. The love of God that is imparted to me compels me to walk in obedience. His love empowers me to do what is right in the sight of the Lord. LOVE takes me to the 'Next Level'."

My prayer for you is that you will embrace the standard of grace. God's grace empowers us to live above sin and unrighteousness. His precious Holy Spirit is here to lead and guide us so that we experience the life of God. Take hold of Him and allow Him to take you to a higher place of living where the law of sin has no dominion and the law of the Spirit reigns. Receive His commandments and allow Him to raise the standard of grace within your life. Let's go to the next level.

ABOUT THE AUTHOR

ROBERT GAY is Senior Pastor and Apostolic founder of High Praise Worship Center in Panama City, Florida. He and his wife Stacey were married in 1981 and today have three children who serve in ministry along with them. Their ministry has a three-fold vision statement: Equipping Believers, Building Families, and Furthering the Kingdom of God. Pastor Robert operates as a prophetic voice that touches thousands nationally and internationally. He is recognized by many as an Apostolic Father bringing balance and order into the church today. For complete bio go to *www.highpraisepc.com.*

HIGH PRAISE
worship center

EQUIPPING BELIEVERS, BUILDING FAMILIES, AND FURTHERING THE KINGDOM OF GOD

FOR MORE INFORMATION ABOUT BOOKS, MUSIC, AND TEACHING CDS BY ROBERT GAY, VISIT US AT: WWW.HIGHPRAISEPC.COM

CONNECT WITH US

FACEBOOK.COM/HIGHPRAISEPC   TWITTER.COM/HIGHPRAISEPC   YOUTUBE.COM/HIGHPRAISEPC

**HIGH PRAISE WORSHIP CENTER
7124 E. HWY. 22
PANAMA CITY, FL 32404**

Parsons Publishing House
Your Voice Your World™

P.O. Box 488, Stafford VA 22554 USA
www.ParsonsPublishingHouse.com
Email: info@ParsonsPublishingHouse.com

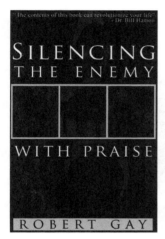

SILENCING THE ENEMY WITH PRAISE
by Robert Gay

Praise is a weapon used to command the enemies in your life to be silent. Robert Gay is known around the world as the father of warfare praise in the Kingdom. In this book, he expands on the Bible truth of praise and how God wants to use praise in your life.
$11.95
ISBN:978-1602730052

70 REASONS FOR SPEAKING IN TONGUES
by Dr. Bill Hamon

Over 600 million Christians have received the Holy Spirit gift of tongues, and 95% of Spirit-baptized Christians only utilize 10% of the benefits of speaking in tongues. Learn how to use your spirit language to activate more faith and increase God's love and power within your life and ministry (216 pages).
$14.95.
ISBN: 978-1602730137

NEXT LEVEL—RAISING THE STANDARD OF GRACE
by Robert Gay

Pastor Robert Gay raises the standard of Scripture against one of the biggest errors of our day. Using Biblical truths, he illuminates many of the common pitfalls that ensnare believers while revealing the true meaning of Grace and its relationship to the Ten Commandments. You are taken on a quest for the grassroots truth that this generation desperately needs for a great awakening.

In this book, Robert is sounding a trumpet call from heaven, engaging the reader to see the Ten Commandments afresh from the empowering view of God's Grace. Robert clearly and biblically explains how Grace takes the Ten Commandments to the "next level" and empowers us to live godly, holy lives above sin. There is no limit to the success, prosperity, and blessings that will surround you when you apply the principles of *Next Level—Raising the Standard of Grace*.

$14.95.

ISBN: 978-1602730427